WRESTLING WITH
LIFE'S TOUGH ISSUES

WRESTLING WITH LIFE'S TOUGH ISSUES

what should a Christian do

CLAIRE DISBREY

HENDRICKSON PUBLISHERS

WRESTLING WITH LIFE'S TOUGH ISSUES: WHAT SHOULD A CHRISTIAN DO?
U.S. edition published by Hendrickson Publishers, Inc.
P. O. Box 3473
Peabody, Massachusetts 01961-3473

Text copyright © 2007 by Claire Disbrey. Original edition published in English under the title *Living in Grace: Virtue Ethics and Christian Living* by The Bible Reading Fellowship, Oxford, England. Copyright © by The Bible Reading Fellowship 2007. U.S. edition published by agreement.

ISBN 978-1-59856-314-6

First printing—November 2008

Cover Art: The Struggle © 2008 Chris Stoffel Overvoorde | Eyekons www.eyekons .com

Library of Congress Cataloging-in-Publication Data

Disbrey, Claire, 1942–
    [Living in grace]
    Wrestling with life's tough issues : what should a Christian do? / Claire Disbrey.—US ed.
        p. cm.
    Originally published: Living in grace. Oxford, England : Bible Reading Fellowship, c2007.
    Includes bibliographical references.
    ISBN 978-1-59856-314-6 (alk. paper)
    1. Christian ethics. 2. Virtue. 3. Ethical problems. 4. Ethics in the Bible. 5. Bible. N.T.—Criticism, interpretation, etc. I. Title.
    BJ1251.D56 2008
    241—dc22
                                                                2008025902

I have come that they may have life, and have it to the full.
(John 10:10)

I would like to thank the church friends who cared for and supported me through the hard times I experienced during the writing of this book.

Contents

SECTION 3: VIRTUE ETHICS EVALUATED

Section 1

Virtue Ethics explained

An introduction to the book

IDEAS ABOUT HOW TO LIVE well are entering a new era; my discovery of this has been one of the most exciting things to happen to me recently. My children used to ask, "Am I allowed?" to go to the store on their own, to use the fire extinguisher, to go through the gate onto the railway crossing. Now they have grown up into an adult world where people don't want to know what the rules are all the time. They still have respect for the laws of the land, however, and can be quite passionate about the importance of virtues like justice, honesty, and kindness.

DOES LOVE MAKE EVERYTHING RIGHT?

A young friend became unexpectedly pregnant. She had some important decisions to make. She wanted to do what was right but wasn't all that impressed by whether or not the church or the state had rules about such things. She was not thinking in terms of rules to keep, but neither was she attracted by the idea that love makes everything right. She tried to imagine what the consequences would be of the various options open to her, but she wanted to go further than that and think seriously about what it was that was growing inside her and which course of action would be fairest to the child that could be born, to its father, and to herself.

A middle-aged couple inherited some money that they weren't expecting and were challenged by a sermon to think about giving some of it away. They discovered that Paul's letters don't point Christians back to the rules laid down in the Old Testament about giving, and responding to their feelings seemed a poor guide. They were, however, impressed by the New Testament idea of becoming more generous people, not only in respect of this money but in every aspect of their lives.

Someone else was wondering if he should remarry after a divorce. He knew that doing what's right is not the same as doing what you feel like, even if the feeling does come from loving someone very deeply, but in order to try to find the right course of action, he was thinking more in terms of the virtues of faithfulness, responsibility, and wisdom than about rules for which he couldn't see the reasons.

Philosophers are calling this new way of thinking "Virtue Ethics" and pointing us back to the thinking of the early Greek world, when people talked more about what it meant to be a good or a bad person than what made an action right or wrong. Some Christians are discovering that this is exactly the point made by Jesus in the Sermon on the Mount (Matthew 5–7) and by Paul in his letters—that living as a Christian is not, at its most basic level, only about obligations and prohibitions, or simply caring about the consequences our actions have for other people. They are discovering that the ethical teaching in the New Testament is not essentially about forbidding certain kinds of behavior—murder, adultery, swearing, and revenge. That's how the Pharisees saw it, and Jesus wanted to set them straight. But neither is it essentially saying, "Just love people and then anything goes." This approach easily sinks into a kind of hedonism that puts pleasure at the center of our thinking. The New Testament approach to living well is, rather, a challenging call to let God's Spirit change the sort of people we are. It is about the quest to become gentle, faithful, honest, self-controlled people.

> *Philosophers are calling this new way of thinking "Virtue Ethics" and pointing us back to the thinking of the early Greek world, when people talked more about what it meant to be a good or a bad person than what made an action right or wrong.*

AN UNCOMFORTABLE SITUATION AND A NEW DISCOVERY

A few years ago, I was teaching a Religious Studies class. We looked at the different philosophical theories about ethics that were around at the time and then tried to fit the teaching of the New Testament into them. It was all very unsatisfactory, and the textbook we were using didn't help us much. It struggled to make some connections, but concluded that biblical ethics includes the ethics both of rules and of love, yet "conforms to neither and to some extent transcends both."[1] Little the philosophers had to say helped us to understand the New Testament, and little that the Bible said helped us to understand the philosophers.

What was Jesus trying to tell his disciples about the law, in the Sermon on the Mount? Do we just need a harder set of rules than the Pharisees had? And what did Paul mean when he said, "Love is the fulfillment of the law" (Romans 13:10)? Does he mean that we should just care about the best outcome for everyone involved and act in the way that seems to us to meet their best interests? Neither of these conclusions—a harder set of rules or acting from love alone—seemed right, and, what was worse, they seemed in many cases to point to quite different ways of behaving.

> *Living well, Aristotle believed, essentially involved not just keeping rules, and not just calculating consequences, but acquiring and practicing virtues.*

When Christians come to the Bible looking for rules about how to behave, they can judge that suicide is always wrong, even when someone seems to have good reasons to take their own life. But when they come to the Bible believing that it teaches them to make judgments out of love for everyone involved, they can conclude that, when the reasons are good enough, suicide is always right. So what are Christians in real ethical dilemmas meant to do?

One evening, at a meeting with some staff of the university I work for, a member of the philosophy department shared with us some new ideas about ethics that had crept into the world of academic philosophy.[2] Instead of putting either rules or consequences at the center of ethics, she took us back to the Greek philosopher Aristotle (384–322 B.C.), who focused his ethics on the idea of virtues. Living well, he believed, essentially involved not just keeping rules, and not just calculating consequences, but acquiring and practicing virtues.

I saw at once that this was what was needed to break through the impasse I had reached. I went back to the Bible, and it was like having a new pair of glasses to look through. Human nature being what it is, when trying to solve our ethical dilemmas, there has always been a tension between looking back to rules (wanting to know what is prohibited and what isn't) and looking forward to consequences (caring about the effects our actions have on others), and the academic moral philosophy of the last two centuries has done nothing but aggravate this tension. Now I could see that the New Testament is not a confusing muddle of these two approaches but is pointing us to a way of "living well" that incorporates them both and integrates them into a larger picture.

Pharisaism and Hedonism

I detect that many Christian people today are disenchanted by what can be seen as the pharisaism of the conservative wing of the Church—the tendency to see, in selected words of the Bible, absolute rules that must be uncompromisingly upheld and applied. They suspect that an ethic based on following rules for which you can't always see the reason is immature and out of step with the culture in which we are now living. More importantly, they see it as a denial both of the mercy and compassion that seem to be at the center of Jesus' life and teaching and of the freedom from the law that Paul spoke about so often. These Christians may be very firmly committed to living by what the Bible says but not convinced that looking for rules is the best way to do it.

Can we take the Christian call to holiness with great seriousness without falling into pharisaism, and take on board the Christian's radical freedom from the law without falling into hedonism?

On the other hand, many Christians are alarmed by what can be seen as the hedonism of the liberal wing of the Church. They are concerned that if there are no absolute rules, there will be no constraint on what people can do: human beings are so hopelessly lost that they are unable to cope with that sort of freedom. If the rules of Christian living can change with changing circumstances and people have only to claim that they are following the path of love, won't their behavior be guided more by what is pleasant than by what is right? What will then be left to make the Christian life distinctive from the surrounding culture? These people feel that the only way to be truly "biblical" and to preserve the distinctiveness of Christian living is to find unchanging rules in the Scriptures and insist that Christians uphold them without being distracted by what is going on in the world around them.

Is there a third way?

So is there a third way? Can we take the Christian call to holiness with great seriousness without falling into pharisaism, and take on board the Christian's radical freedom from the law without falling into hedonism?

I believe now that there is such a way. I have come to see that approaching the teaching of the New Testament through the ideas of Virtue Ethics can expose the pharisaism that Jesus was so much against because it excluded people

wrestling with life's tough issues

from the kingdom of heaven (Matthew 23). It can also help us to rediscover the freedom of Paul's ethics in which "everything is permissible" (1 Corinthians 6:12; 10:23), but at the same time everything is constrained by the pursuit of Christian character, described by Paul as "love, joy, peace, patience, kindness, goodness, faithfulness, gentleness and self-control" (Galatians 5:22–23).

In this book, I want to explain and explore this "new" approach to the ethical teaching of the New Testament. In fact, it is not a new approach at all but an old one, which has become obscured by the work of academic moral philosophy within the movement known as "modernity." Modernity is a way of thinking that developed in Western Europe in the 17th century, which displaced faith in God from the centre of our thinking, replacing it with faith in the ability of human rationality to answer all our questions and solve all our problems. At the same time, it turned the focus of ethical discussion away from the behavior of corporations and states and toward the behavior of individuals.

Some readers may be wondering why Christians need concern themselves with the secular world of academic philosophy. Can't we just read the Bible for ourselves and put into practice what we read? But the fact is that although we may not be aware of it, the way ordinary Christians approach the Bible today and interpret what they read is already, to a large extent, determined by what has gone on in the world of academic philosophy in the past. The polarization between the ethics of rules and the ethics of consequences that has distracted and fragmented the secular world has distracted and fragmented the theological world too, and the different traditions of ethical thinking have become as polarized in the church as they are elsewhere.

I believe that returning to the idea of virtue may not only be a way for the church to disentangle some of its present conflicts and work toward presenting a united, distinctive Christian ethic to the world, but it might also point a way toward a much-needed universal ethic for a pluralist world, one that can be welcomed and embraced by the world's religions as well as its secular institutions.

The book is not addressed to theologians or philosophers (although there are footnotes to help those who would like to make connections and take things further). It is addressed to ordinary Christians who want to live by the Bible and heal the divisions that damage the church and its witness to the world.

WAYS OF USING THE BIBLE

This is essentially a book about how to use the Bible. It is for people who believe (or perhaps would like to believe) that when we come to the Bible as members of an ongoing community of believers, with our minds in gear and praying for the guidance of God's Holy Spirit, we find not only the challenge and inspiration but also the practical help and direction that we need to live well.

I believe that many Christians who face real dilemmas and want to do what is right turn to the Bible for help or ask other Christians for guidance, and end up confused, because the Bible seems to say different things. Even biblical scholars appear unable to agree on how to make sense of it all.

This book will explore what happens when a group of fictitious people—each facing a specific moral dilemma and genuinely wanting to know what is the right, distinctively Christian course of action—turn to the Bible for help. It will, perhaps rather artificially, separate out three approaches to ethics, which many people try to use together, with differing emphases and differing outcomes. How the stories end will depend on which of these approaches they bring to their reading of the Bible—what they are looking for as they search for guidance on what to do.

People who approach the Bible looking for quite different things sometimes seem to be shouting at each other across a huge void. It is often not the case that one side is more "biblical" or more ready to be obedient than the other, but just that people are approaching the Bible with different interpretative tools.

If we are confused about what we are looking for, we shall find conflicting answers. Does the Bible, for example, lay down the absolute rule that divorced people may not remarry, whatever the consequences, or that people may not take their own lives whatever the circumstances? Or does it, on the other hand, tell us that in these sorts of situations we should let love be our only guide and take whatever course of action secures the best outcome for everyone involved? And if we approach the Bible from a different angle altogether, considering the virtues that it sets before us, will that lead us more clearly toward Christian holiness? What will happen if we concentrate our thinking not on right or wrong actions but on good and bad people? Can the Bible provide us with clear ideas about the virtues or vices that we should pursue in these kinds of situations, and will this be of practical help in the complex questions of real life?

We shall be looking quite closely at some real-life situations and different ways of interpreting particular passages of the Bible. All the people in these

> *If we approach the Bible from a different angle altogether, considering the virtues that it sets before us, will that lead us more clearly toward Christian holiness?*

wrestling with life's tough issues

dilemmas will genuinely want to know what the Bible says and to be obedient to it, and we shall see what happens when they approach the Bible looking for rules, or looking at consequences, or looking for virtues.

TOWARD UNITY AND DISTINCTIVENESS

My hope is that the old insights of Virtue Ethics can help Christians to get beyond a state of confusion and conflict and move toward a way of seeing the ethical teaching of the New Testament as a coherent and eminently practical whole. I hope that this will help Christian people of different temperaments and from different traditions to begin to discern and agree on a distinctively Christian way of living in the contemporary world.

Can the Bible provide us with clear ideas about the virtues or vices that we should pursue in these kinds of situations, and will this be of practical help in the complex questions of real life?

Before considering these stories of Christian people like me, and perhaps you, who find themselves faced with decisions about divorce, suicide, honesty, abortion, war, and possessions, we will dip into the world of philosophy to see how Virtue Ethics was rediscovered.

1

How the philosophers muddied the waters

ALMOST EVERYONE IN THE WORLD grows up with the idea that some ways of behaving are right and some are wrong. The adult students of all ages and from many different backgrounds who attend the classes I run for the Open University, a distance learning school in Great Britain, are no exception. I sometimes ask them for examples of actions that they think they ought, or ought not, to do. They suggest: "I ought to pay my bus fare"; "I ought to give money to poverty relief agencies"; "I ought not cheat in my exams"; "I ought not flirt with my friend's husband."

If I then go on to ask them why they think these ways of behaving are right or wrong, they come up with a whole variety of reasons: "I think I just know some things are right"; "I would feel bad if I did it"; "I was brought up to know the difference between right and wrong"; "It's against the law"; "I believe rules like the Ten Commandments are a good basis for civilized life"; "It would lead to trouble for other people as well as myself"; "I can see that rules like this are necessary for social life to run smoothly"; "It wouldn't be fair"; "I think faithfulness, or generosity, is important."

On the whole, these students agree. If they don't—if one of them is a vegetarian, for example—they may attempt to defend the way they feel, but in the end they are usually happy to accept that people have been brought up differently or value different things.

This may be a rather simplistic picture of how a cross-section of ordinary people from several generations make moral decisions, and how they feel about the moral decisions of others. It is not the whole story, of course. In 2003, for instance, many thousands of people felt strongly enough about the invasion of Iraq by armies from the United States and Great Britain to take part in peace marches, and others have, in smaller numbers, campaigned vigorously for a ban on animals being used for experiments, for debt relief for poor countries, or for better protection of the environment.

This week, our local paper has a front page picture of protesters gathered up and around an ancient and dangerous tree in our pastor's garden. They were successful in stopping it being felled, and the paper commended them for "caring enough about their own back yard to get things done"—or in this case, of course, not done.

The media paint a less rosy, if sometimes unfair, picture of how Christians make their moral decisions and what they feel about the morality of their fellow believers. The difference is that Christians have the Bible, and many years of its study and interpretation, to help them, but they do not agree on how to use it. Some Christians look more to church traditions, to their own reason, or to the Holy Spirit's guidance of the individual than to the Bible for guidance, but even those who are genuinely committed to living by the Bible don't agree about how to use it.

Looking for rules

As we saw in the introduction to this section, one school of thought looks mainly for rules. This reflects the ideas of the German philosopher Immanuel Kant (1724–1804),[3] or perhaps a particular interpretation of his philosophy, which says that living well consists of keeping universally binding rules, regardless of the consequences.

To look at an example, there is clearly some sort of rule in the Bible against taking life, against killing (Exodus 20:13). Actually it is a rule against murder, which does not cover all killing. At the time the rule was given, killing animals was allowed for food (Genesis 9:3) and for sacrifice (Leviticus 4:14–15), and so was killing fellow human beings in legitimate wars (Joshua 6:17) and in punishment for certain offenses (Exodus 21:12). Christians who start their moral thinking from the rules they find in the Bible have to decide if killing a fox for sport, or a laboratory rat, or a lamb for food now come into the category of murder—illegal killing. They have to decide if the biblical rule applies now to a convicted criminal or to a fetus, to taking their own life or helping someone who wants to die.

Some Christians, for example, argue that a human fetus is the epitome of innocent, powerless human life, and so they put an absolute prohibition on abortion, whatever the consequences. This is a valid way of using the Bible to make moral decisions: extending rules by analogy is one of the main methods that rabbis use to interpret the Torah in new situations.

Slipping into pharisaism

A rule-based approach like this can be used in a flexible and compassionate way. Rules that are seen to be derived from Scripture, such as the ban imposed

wrestling with life's tough issues

by an early church council on eating non-kosher meat (recorded in Acts 15), or the Church's later ban on taking interest on loans, on suicide, on the ordination of women, and on divorce, can be applied with mercy. They can be seen to be open to change with changing circumstances and with the ongoing guidance of God's Spirit in the Church.

A rule-based approach like this can be used in a flexible and compassionate way. . . . The danger is, however, that without such flexibility and compassion this way of approaching ethics can slip over into pharisaism.

Thomas Aquinas (1225–1274) is an example of this sort of flexibility. As one of the Christian Church's formative ethical thinkers, he believed that the content of the natural law (moral rules that could be derived from the very nature of human beings), which he thought should guide Christian behavior, would change as people's knowledge and circumstances changed.[4]

The danger is, however, that without such flexibility and compassion this way of approaching ethics can slip over into pharisaism. Jesus said that when absolute rules are applied uncompromisingly, without the virtues of justice, mercy, and faithfulness, people are kept out of the kingdom of heaven, because this way of thinking enables some to feel self-righteous and others to feel impossibly burdened (Matthew 23).

LOOKING FOR CONSEQUENCES

The other school of thought looks mainly at consequences. People who follow this way of thinking may be no less concerned to do what the Bible says, but may give more attention to such passages as Jesus' summary of the Commandments (loving God with all your being, and loving your neighbor as yourself: Luke 10:27) and to Paul's comment that Christians have only one debt outstanding, "the continuing debt to love one another," for "love is the fulfillment of the law" (Romans 13:8, 10).

Those who use this approach come to each situation on the basis of wanting to express love—an impartial and benevolent concern for everyone who will be affected by the actions they take. It takes some calculation and some balancing, but in the end the right thing to do emerges as whatever brings the best outcome for everyone.

When thinking about a particular case of an unwanted pregnancy, for example, people looking at the consequences of their actions would want to calculate the misery and cost of an unwanted baby—perhaps especially an unwanted disabled baby—to all those intimately affected and to society in general. They would then compare this with the pain and dangers of a termination for the mother and the costs for her and for others, including the child who might have been born, and in each separate case come up with an answer that flows from love.

Slipping into hedonism

Clearly, these sorts of calculations are an important element in moral decision-making. The danger is that any consequence-based ethic can slip over into hedonism. When we act from love, we strive to do the best for everyone, and it is hard for this not to become simply acting in the way that takes away people's pain and makes them happy—just balancing what we want for ourselves with what we believe others want for themselves. Pleasure, or what we might call personal happiness, can then easily become our guiding thought, and other principles such as the sanctity of all created life, the requirements of justice or the need for trust can get overlooked.

> *Clearly, these sorts of calculations are an important element in moral decision-making. The danger is that any consequence-based ethic can slip over into hedonism.*

CHRISTIANS AT WAR

People see these two groups of Christians at war with one another. They see people who describe themselves as Christians disagreeing in the most fundamental, wide-ranging, and often hostile way about one issue after another—women's roles, abortion, divorce, war, homosexuality—shouting at each other across a void of misunderstanding and accusing the other camp of being "unbiblical" and even "unchristian."

In a letter to the newspaper I read, a Christian in training for ministry commented on a sermon preached by the Archbishop of Canterbury at the institution of a celibate homosexual as Dean of a cathedral. He accused the archbishop of "showing no signs of being a Christian because his Jesus is merely one to be followed like one might admire a poet." If any good can come out of sermons like these, he continued, "It is only because Dr. Williams

wrestling with life's tough issues

provides such a clear example of false religion that we are compelled to describe and preach the opposite." In a later letter, another Christian said it was no wonder that the Church of England was emptying when a new breed of Anglicans were "using the Bible like a Delia Smith[5] cookbook."

How did this polarization come about, and what can be done to show the world that there is a distinctively Christian way of living—a way that is firmly based on the Bible, a way that can break down the barriers that keep people apart and commend the good news of Jesus to a skeptical world?

IDEAS ABOUT GOODNESS

It was the ancient Greeks who first started to ask questions about morality and attempt to construct theories about it. At the beginning of this period, defining the qualities of good rulers, farmers, or slaves was like defining the qualities of good knives or oxen. Objects and people were good if they fit the role they had to play and performed it efficiently, so that the life of the community could proceed harmoniously.

As Greek society underwent some significant changes in the 5th century B.C., some Greek thinkers[6] began to try to define a good person in more general terms. They asked what qualities people needed in order to flourish as human beings, to have worthwhile, satisfying lives—but always in the context of a particular kind of society. Jesus was concerned with these questions too. He said, "Blessed [or happy] are the poor in spirit, for theirs is the kingdom of heaven. . . . Blessed are the pure in heart, for they will see God" (Matthew 5:3, 8). He said, "No one who puts his hand to the plow and looks back is fit for service in the kingdom of God" (Luke 9:62), and, "I have come that they may have life, and have it to the full" (John 10:10).

What can be done to show the world that there is a distinctively Christian way of living—a way that is firmly based on the Bible, a way that can break down the barriers that keep people apart and commend the good news of Jesus to a skeptical world?

So how did the idea of becoming a certain kind of person in order to pursue a flourishing life then get replaced with "doing your duty" even if it made you miserable? How did the idea of developing virtuous qualities get replaced with calculating the consequences that bring the most happiness, and how did the idea of an individual acting alone come to replace the idea of living in a good community? The story is a long and complicated one[7] that runs through Augustine (354–430), Aquinas (c.1226–1274), and Luther (1483–1546).

One modern philosopher has said that the main misfortune that led to the demise of the virtue approach was Christianity.[8] As Christianity changed from being a small charismatic community to being a huge (Roman) institution,[9] its morality of virtue (the pursuit of a holy character) became a morality of duty, the pursuit of actions that complied with the rules of the Church. Thomas Aquinas turned back to Aristotle to work out his theology of natural law— rules that could be derived from the idea of a good human life—but from then on, Roman Catholic morality became focused mainly on defining specific acts that were, or were not, prohibited. In a move that went against most of the apostle Paul's calls to distinctive Christian living, "virtues" became the personal characteristics that led people to obey the commands of the law.

OBEYING THE BIBLE

The Protestant Reformers emphasized the idea that all human desire and speculation were corrupt; the individual was personally responsible before God and entirely dependent for salvation on his grace. Luther reacted against the legalism of the Roman Church and encouraged Christians to read the Bible for themselves. Moral living in the Reformed Churches became largely a matter, for Christians, of turning their back on their desires and obeying what they read in the Bible, without questioning or expecting any advantages from doing so.

The continued growth of individualism finally buried the idea that good people were those who had the qualities to play the part that society allotted them, and so find fulfillment and harmony in their work and in their relationships. The connection between happiness and duty also disappeared. To pursue happiness was now to neglect your duty, and to pursue duty was to be careless of your own and other people's happiness.

When the Enlightenment[10] began to take a hold, and the philosophers and theorists in the Western world were no longer prepared to live by unthinking obedience to institutions or revelation from divine beings, one major philosopher chose to go down the route of duty and another down the route of happiness.

IMMANUEL KANT

As a man of the Enlightenment, Immanuel Kant (1724–1804) believed that human reason, the ability to think about issues and come up with

wrestling with life's tough issues

the right answers, was unique and universal. If, then, a set of moral rules could be reached by reason alone, reasonable people all over the world would recognize that those rules were unconditionally binding upon everyone.

Virtue Ethics points us toward another biblical truth: that a community committed to right living—to justice, faithfulness, gentleness, and honesty—will generally be a better place in which to live.

Kant argued that the only thing in the world that is unconditionally good is the will to do what is right. So he proposed that people are good only insofar as they perform actions for the sake of duty alone, denying all desires, inclinations, and self-interest, and ignoring any consequences.

Using his own reasoning powers, Kant proposed a way of arriving at a set of rules that distinguished right actions from wrong and that everyone had a duty to keep. Good people—those who live by duty—might well have miserable lives this side of death, but, Kant believed, God would crown virtue with happiness in the next life.

A contemporary Christian expression of this sort of approach can be seen in R. C. Sproul's *Right and Wrong*.[11] Sproul says that taking comfort in divine revelation is a risky business, "because the presence of hostility in the human heart to the rule of God makes for conflict between divine precepts and human desires."[12] "Doing what love demands, what Christ commands, often means the bearing of unspeakable suffering."[13]

While Jesus' death on the cross shows us that this last sentence can be true for an individual, Virtue Ethics points us toward another biblical truth: that a community committed to right living—to justice, faithfulness, gentleness, and honesty—will generally be a better place in which to live.[14]

JOHN STUART MILL

The English philosopher John Stuart Mill (1806–1873) took over a theory developed by his teacher and friend Jeremy Bentham (1748–1832) and honed it into another theory about how to decide what actions we ought to take, a theory that is quite different from Kant's.[15]

Bentham was a hedonist: he used his reason to come to the conclusion that only pleasure is good in itself and that pain is the sole thing that is bad in itself. Virtues like kindness and honesty are valuable only insofar as they increase the pleasure and decrease the pain in the world. He therefore proposed that the two experiences of pleasure and pain are all we need to guide us toward ethical living. We should judge all our actions not by referring to universal rules that we have a duty to keep, but by whichever actions bring more pleasure into the world.

Mill took over this idea but made a distinction between different sorts of pleasure. Arguing that "it is better to be a human being dissatisfied than a pig satisfied," and that "if the fool, or the pig, is of a differing opinion, it is because they only know their own side of the question,"[16] he proposed that what he called "the higher pleasures"—the pleasures of the intellect—were more intrinsically valuable than the pleasures

> *Mill argues that "it is better to be a human being dissatisfied than a pig satisfied."*

of the body, and that to live well was therefore to live in a way that maximized the higher pleasures and minimized the pain in the world. Moral rules can be useful insofar as they serve to make people happy, but they shouldn't be followed blindly. If the consequences of breaking a moral rule would lead to more happiness, then keeping it would be the wrong thing to do.

According to this theory, our own happiness always has to be balanced with the happiness of everyone else affected by our behavior. This may seriously curtail the pursuit of our own pleasure, but most of the proponents of this approach claim that this is, in fact, the most satisfying and pleasurable way of living as a human being.

In the 1960s, the Anglican bishop John A. T. Robinson (1919–1983) enthusiastically embraced the ideas of Joseph Fletcher (1905–1991),[17] an American Episcopalian, who suggested that Christians should put people before principles. Adapting Mill's ideas about using the consequences of our actions to come to decisions about the right things to do, Fletcher suggested that Christians should take only the commandment to love as an absolute moral principle. They should examine every situation in which they found themselves to decide how the virtue of love should best be applied in that case. In his book *Honest to God* Robinson had a chapter called "The New Morality," in which one of the subtitles was "Nothing prescribed—except love."[18]

Both Kant's and Mill's philosophical theories about how to decide which actions are right and which are wrong have much to commend them, but, while there are clear difficulties with both when they are applied on their own, the contradictions in the foundations on which they are based make it hard to bring them together. For many years, philosophers have tried

wrestling with life's tough issues

to do this, but it seems inevitable that they end up siding with either one or the other.

CONSERVATIVES AND LIBERALS

In the Christian world, this divide has to some extent fit in with the divide between a conservative approach, which wants to keep things how they are and have things stated clearly, and a liberal approach, which wants to move with the times and is happy with ambiguity. Both conservatives and liberals can look into the Bible and, seeing through their own particular glasses, find passages that confirm their preferred point of view.

This is because the ethics of the Bible is a curious mixture of both and neither of these theories, which is not surprising, since it was written long before the philosophers muddied the waters—before duty and pleasure were parted and rules and consequences were set against each other, before moral living became focused on the right and wrong actions of individuals rather than the virtues and vices of people living in communities.

There are signs of a recovery. In 1980, the writers of the Church of England's *Alternative Service Book* decided on this happy translation of Cranmer's old prayer: "It is indeed right, it is our duty and our joy, at all times and in all places to give you thanks and praise, holy Father, heavenly King . . ."[19]

The rediscovery of Virtue Ethics

In 1958, Elizabeth Anscombe, a respected British philosopher and a Christian, published a paper in a prominent philosophical journal.[20] She suggested that moral philosophy, as it was done in British universities, should be abandoned, because nothing profitable was emerging from it. She was very critical of Kant's suggestion that people could make up laws for themselves and of Mill's idea that there was nothing that consequences could not make right. Although it was a long time before this paper had any significant effect on what philosophers were doing, it has since been seen as a sort of watershed in academic moral philosophy.

During most of the 19th and 20th centuries, the majority of academics working in the field of moral philosophy looked back to the basic ideas of either Kant or Mill (some would say, to Kant and Mill as they had been understood rather than as they actually were).[21] They saw ethics either in terms of duty—of helping people find rules that would guide them toward the right behavior (but not necessarily finding happiness)—or in terms of general happiness—calculating the consequences of their actions

> *During most of the 19th and 20th centuries, the majority of academics . . . saw ethics either in terms of duty—of helping people find rules that would guide them toward the right behavior (but not necessarily finding happiness)—or in terms of general happiness— calculating the consequences of their actions (and not being constrained by anything other than rather vague notions of love or pleasure).*

(and not being constrained by anything other than rather vague notions of love or pleasure). Although attempts were made to bring these two approaches together, they had become so polarized that none of the attempts was generally judged to have worked very satisfactorily. At the bottom line, judgments were made either in terms of rules or in terms of consequences, and the results were often quite different, so not very much practical help was available to people in real dilemmas.

Throughout this period, those involved in the main streams of religious thought, insofar as they were aware of Western academic philosophy, absorbed this polarization to some extent. All the major religions of the world have some ideas about revealed rules. They all also believe, in some form, that overcoming the central influence of the ego is the main ethical task, and part of this task is characteristically seen as developing compassion for others.

The religions of the world, however, add another dimension to moral living—the idea of good and evil, and belief in the basic human ability to discern them in a rather more direct way than the philosophers propose.[22] In fact, the religions would say that this ability to recognize values such as beauty, goodness, truth, wisdom, and love is one of the characteristics that makes us human beings (some would add, created in the image of God) and gives our lives meaning and significance. To connect with the source of these values, and to pursue them within a distinctive community, will fulfill our deepest needs and desires and lead us to the only authentic and ultimately satisfying way of living.

Values and goals

Both Kant's ethics of duty and Mill's ethics of happy consequences became detached from the idea that the moral life is based on specific values and has specific goals or ends. Kant directs us to pursue duty for duty's sake, being careless of the consequences, and Mill directs us to pursue the general happiness—an idea that, in spite of Mill's thoughts about "higher pleasures," has very little content beyond what people desire (not at all the same thing as what people ought to desire if they are to live good lives). Neither of them asks why we ought to live this way.

Jesus, in the Sermon on the Mount, brings together the idea of happiness (blessedness) with values (things that are worth pursuing for their own sake), and he says that, as part of God's redeemed community, we ought to strive for moral perfection, because our heavenly Father is perfect (Matthew 5:1–12, 48).

It is odd, then, though perhaps not surprising, that when academic philosophers began to turn back to Aristotle and think about the meaning of "a good life" and how we ought to live in order to achieve it, Christian thinkers were divided about the usefulness of the idea.

wrestling with life's tough issues

In the academic paper that initiated the debate, Elizabeth Anscombe's main argument was that the differences between the two currently competing approaches to ethics were actually of little importance. This was because all the moral philosophy that had been done in England since the turn of the century was based on the legalistic notion of obligation. Either we had to obey the laws that reason dictated or we had to obey the principle of pursuing the greatest happiness.

Anscombe argued that this notion of obligation made no sense in a secular culture. European philosophical ethics had developed in the Christian era, in a culture where there was believed to be a divine law giver who was above all human institutions and laws, but then it had, as it were, lost the plot. Kant and Mill, and those who followed them, had given up on the idea of a law giver but held on to the idea of being under a legal obligation to act in a particular way.

Anscombe suggested that to get moral philosophy back on track, it should return to Aristotle and the idea of moral virtue.

She suggested that to get moral philosophy back on track, it should return to Aristotle and the idea of moral virtue. Moral philosophers should start talking again about good people instead of right actions, and base their discussions not on the idea of obligation but, as Aristotle did, on the idea of human flourishing, of a life worth living and the traits of character necessary to achieve one.

Anscombe's paper provoked much opposition and a vigorous defense of modern moral philosophy, but it struck a chord with some people working in the field. Slowly, other papers began to appear, pointing out some of the failures in the present way of thinking and some of the advantages of starting over again.[23] It was a slow process, and it was not until the 1990s that Virtue Ethics was being generally recognized as a serious rival to the existing moral theories and as one of the most promising developments in ethics, even if it had by then become a development from Aristotle rather than a simple rediscovery of his ideas.

Virtue Ethics explored

Virtue Ethics was recommended as a way of putting behind us the tensions between duty or happiness, and rules or consequences, and embarking on finding a way to incorporate all these factors in moral decision-making—a way that did not produce conflicting, abstract guidance but real help, to real people, in real moral dilemmas. A new polarization began to emerge in the world of secular moral philosophy between ethical theories that were based on the idea of obligation, to either rules or principles derived from human reason, and ethical theories that were based on people's motives and characters.

More philosophers began to argue that when you stand back and look at how people actually make moral decisions, and at what we generally consider to be admirable behavior, motives become at least as important as actions, and the motive to act well is produced far more often from a good character than from an intellectual exercise or a strong will. We admire people when they act well because they are kind or honest or generous people, not because they are able to apply sets of rules or calculate a set of consequences out of a sense of duty.

We admire people when they act well because they are kind or honest or generous people, not because they are able to apply sets of rules or calculate a set of consequences out of a sense of duty.

If someone visits you in the hospital, you are more pleased and probably admire them more if you know that they are motivated by friendship—because they care that you feel bored and anxious in a hospital—than if you suspect they are acting out of a sense of obligation.

While circumstances can sometimes make it hard to do the right thing, we do not usually think it hard for an honest woman to refrain from taking items off the supermarket shelves without paying. Such behavior would not even enter her head, and it is this harmony between a person's nature and actions that we admire: this sort of integrated living is commonly judged to be the mark of a genuinely good person.

Was this not the very point that Jesus was making in the Sermon on the Mount, when he said that lust was as important as adultery, and anger was as important as murder? For Jesus' followers, motive and character matter as much as actions, because we are called to be holy people who reflect the nature of our God, not just in our behavior but in our being.

Virtuous people characteristically behave well because they value the right things, things such as friendship and family ties and community, and value them not just in their heads but in their hearts, in a way that is expressed both in what they feel and in what they do. They act well because they value people rather than principles, and they value those people for their own sake rather than as objects of duty. They sense that a good human life is a life lived

wrestling with life's tough issues

in harmony with other people, and these values enable them to distinguish what is trivial in life from what is serious and worthwhile.

A "moral saint"

One of the problems discovered with both Kant's and Mill's ethical theories was that if you imagine someone who is morally perfect by their lists of authoritative rules, you actually find a rather unattractive life. There is an awkward split between reasons and motives and between feelings and actions. For someone who, according to their thinking, might be considered a moral saint, reasons for acting well will center on abstract principles and will not be connected with natural bonds like parenthood, friendship, and membership of a community.

LOVING YOURSELF

It was also noticed that, with both the old schemes, there is a sense in which a person's own well-being slips into the background or disappears altogether. Taking care of ourselves is at best allowed, to be balanced equally with taking care of all the other people who will be affected by our actions. If living well comes from valuing other people for their own sake, however, it could—it should—come from valuing the people closest to us in a special way and from valuing our own life too.

Keeping to the rules in every situation, or always acting to maximize happiness, might leave little room for the pursuit of inner harmony, loving relationships, and good friends, for taking pleasure in the natural world or the arts and developing skills and talents for their own sake. Because Virtue Ethics begins with the idea of human life at its best, it can move from activities like these to see that the qualities of character necessary to achieve a flourishing life include virtues like integrity,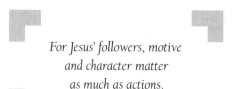

For Jesus' followers, motive and character matter as much as actions.

gratitude, honesty, generosity, faithfulness, and patience—the very virtues that Paul recommends to Christians in his letters.

Acquiring these qualities may not always bring direct benefit to the individual. On the contrary, in certain circumstances it might lead to opposition and suffering. It is clear, however, that living in a community without those qualities falls far short of any idea of human life at its best. Having recently fallen victim to a scam, I am only too well aware of how inconvenient and miserable it is to live in a society where trust seems to be dwindling.

Personal qualities to cope with complex situations

Virtue Ethics seemed to many to capture in a more realistic way the experience of moral living—the feeling that it must be more deeply complex than using the intellect to discern and apply good rules or principles, that it requires personal qualities like sensitivity, discernment, perception, and wisdom, which grow from good models and from practice and come only with personal maturity. No set of rules or principles could capture what a virtuous person would do in a complex situation, but the fact that there may be more than one right answer to every dilemma does not mean that our own and other people's actions cannot be evaluated as just or unjust, kind or cruel, mean or generous.

> *One of the problems discovered with both Kant's and Mill's ethical theories was that if you imagine someone who is morally perfect by their lists of authoritative rules, you actually find a rather unattractive life.*

Some women philosophers embraced Virtue Ethics as a chance to see morality in terms of caring relationships, rather than what they saw as a male preoccupation with justice and self-reliance. Others have seen it as a chance to move not only toward a different kind of ethics but also toward a different kind of society, and have explored its implications for politics and business, and for social issues like abortion and the care of the elderly.[24]

Virtue Ethics still has its critics and its opponents, its difficulties and its failures. It will keep academic philosophers in work for many years to come, but it has certainly stirred the world of moral philosophy into new life.

CHRISTIAN RESPONSES TO VIRTUE ETHICS

Virtue Ethics is self-consciously an ethic for a secular world. (It is also part of the current move away from the influence of the Enlightenment.) I think it is significant, therefore, that the two people who have been most responsible for its rediscovery are Christians: Elizabeth Anscombe (who died in 2001) and Alasdair MacIntyre[25] are both Roman Catholics.

In his early writings, MacIntyre was rather dismissive of New Testament ethics, but, in a new preface to his *Short History of Ethics* in 1998, he says he has come to see that the New Testament defines a life for Christians informed both by the hope of the second coming and by "a commitment to this-worldly activity in and through which human beings rediscover the true nature of their natural ends and of those natural virtues required to achieve those ends, as a result of coming to understand them in the light of theological virtues identified in the New Testament." He continues by saying that those virtues are "the qualities necessary for obedience to God's law."[26]

Some other Christian thinkers also responded warmly. Stanley Hauerwas, for example, used the new approach to explore what we can learn from God's revelation in Jesus Christ about the sort of community the Christian Church should be, and about the virtues Christians need in order to take part in it and sustain it.[27]

Others have not been so welcoming. In an article in *Studies in Christian Ethics*, John Barton outlines what he sees as the four features that people have in mind when they talk about Virtue Ethics and goes on to say, "To begin, then . . . it would seem that there is no virtue ethics in the Bible."[28] Later he says, "Thus it seems to me that the language of 'virtue' may not be well adapted to describe the Old Testament's characteristic approaches to morality, which the old models of deontology [the ethics of rules] and consequentialism are better at describing."[29] John Barton admits that the Old Testament is what he knows about, but he extends his conclusion to cover Jesus' and Paul's ethics and the teaching of the early Church. He ends by saying, "It is certainly worth asking about virtue in the Bible and interesting possibilities are opened up by doing so."[30]

I hope that the stories in the rest of this book will open up some of those "interesting possibilities" to people who may not know very much about moral philosophy or who have not come across the Virtue Ethics approach before.

Three ways of approaching the Bible

BEFORE WE START LOOKING AT some examples of people using the New Testament in situations where they face ethical dilemmas, it will be helpful to sum up the three ethical approaches that I will refer to in the case studies.

RULE-BASED APPROACHES

The main feature of rule-based approaches to ethics is that they make a link between right actions and moral rules or principles, which are usually seen to be universal or absolute: that is, they apply to every person in every situation that might arise. Living well is about doing our duty, and deciding on the right course of action in a particular situation will focus primarily on asking questions about rules: Where can I find good rules? Are there any rules that apply in this case? If there is a conflict between several rules that all apply, how can I best resolve it? Put formally, an action is right if, and only if, it is in accordance with a correct moral rule. Two examples of such moral rules are that adultery is wrong and that it is right to preserve human life.

> *The main feature of rule-based approaches to ethics is that they make a link between right actions and moral rules or principles.*

Since these approaches are based on the idea of good rules, thought needs to be given to where we can find good rules and how we know that they are good. Rules may be seen as correct because they have been revealed by a deity or revered teacher, or because they are enshrined in authoritative writings or the traditions of an institution or culture. The Ten Commandments are a good example.

Rules and cultures

Another way of arriving at correct rules is to use the idea of natural law. Some moral laws are thought to be evident to any member of the human race because, for example, our consciences inform us, or because they can be argued from human biology. The rule that homosexual acts are wrong is sometimes defended using this idea. The apostle Paul uses this sort of argument when he says in 1 Corinthians 11:14, "Does not the very nature of things teach you . . ." The fact that he is arguing here that for a man to have long hair is "a disgrace to him" leads some Christians to believe that these sorts of arguments are sometimes conditioned more by culture than by reason.

If people use some of these methods to choose sets of rules, different faith communities or cultures may end up having differences of opinion about what is right. Some people would argue, however, that some sets of rules can be shown to be correct by the exercise of reason alone. They would say, for example, that every reasonable person can see that lying must be wrong, because if everyone always lied, social life would be impossible. This argument may lead to a rule, but not necessarily to a reason for keeping it, as not everyone may value social life!

Discovering our duty

According to these approaches, deciding on a course of action in a particular situation will involve finding out what our duty is—using our minds to identify the universal rules that apply. Are any of the actions open to us prohibited? For example, does that particular action count as fornication or idolatry? Is this a sort of killing that is allowed or not? If there is a conflict between rules, we may have to prioritize and balance them. Is it more important to tell the truth or to protect someone from harm? Would it be right to kill this person, or that animal, if many other lives might be saved as a result? Once we have decided what our duty is, we then need the strength of will to do it.

Obligations and prohibitions are experienced as imposed on us from the outside, and we may have to deny our own feelings and natural inclinations if they conflict with the obligations. According to this approach, the best motive to have is the will to do what is right, regardless of the possible cost to ourselves or to others.

Judging others

When ethics are seen in this way, it can appear relatively straightforward to judge whether an action is right or wrong, without reference to a person's

wrestling with life's tough issues

motives or character or to the details of the situation. If the rule has not been kept, the behavior is reprehensible.

It is possible to use a rule-based approach but to identify only general rules, for which there may be many exceptions. We could say that it is generally right to tell the truth or be faithful to our spouse, but there may be situations in which this rule does not apply—if, for example, lying to an assailant about the whereabouts of their victim or sleeping with a prison guard would save someone else's life. We could think of different sorts of rules stacked into priority schemes or judged to be good on the basis of the consequences of

Approaches to ethics based not on rules but on consequences make a link between right actions and the consequences of those actions.

keeping them, but, if the idea remains that it is moral rules that make actions right or wrong, then the approach can be categorized as rule-based.

Christians who see ethics in this way come to the Bible looking for universal rules in the various writings of the Old Testament, in the words of Jesus, and in the letters written by the early Church leaders, and there is a tendency to judge other Christians who fail to live by the rules found there. Some other Christians criticize this approach as reflecting neither the complexity of some situations nor the Bible's revelation of a loving God who wants us to have life "to the full" (John 10:10) and calls us to love one another—to be generous, merciful, and compassionate.

CONSEQUENCE-BASED APPROACHES

Approaches to ethics based not on rules but on consequences make a link between right actions and the consequences of those actions. These approaches are often equated with an ethic of love because they suggest that our actions should be guided by an equal care about the well-being of everyone who will be affected by them. Living well is about caring about the well-being of others as much as we care about our own.

Deciding the right course of action in a specific situation is, however, not a matter of exploring our feelings but of making impartial calculations. How will my actions affect John? How will they affect Joan? Is the harm here outweighed by the good there? What course of action will minimize harm and maximize good overall? Put formally, an action is deemed right if, and only if, it promotes the best outcome for everyone affected by it. Whether it would be right to tell a lie in some particular situation, for example, will depend on how much harm would be avoided and how much good done by acting in this way.

Since these approaches are based on the idea of good outcomes, some thought clearly needs to be given to what counts as a good outcome. It is usually agreed that frustrating what people want, denying them what they need, or causing them distress or pain are harmful outcomes, while giving them what they want or need or increasing their happiness and well-being are good outcomes.

Consequences and cultures

The single term most often used for calculating a good outcome is "personal happiness," but clearly what counts as a good outcome varies among people from different cultures or with different worldviews—different ideas about the meaning and destiny of human lives. For Christians, the Bible is a useful guide in answering these sorts of questions.

Having a loving nature may make it easier to live well according to these approaches. In the end, however, it is a matter of having the mental skills and imagination to think through the likely consequences and balance them against each other, and the strength of will to do what is right when the right decision emerges, even if it breaks traditional rules or does not provide the best outcome for ourselves.

Judging others

While other people's actions may be criticized as selfish or likely to cause more harm than good, consequence-based approaches will usually involve a greater understanding of the complexity of moral decision-making and of the need to appreciate the whole situation before making a judgment.

Christians who see ethics in this way will focus on New Testament passages about the importance of love. They will see the lives and teachings of Jesus and the apostles as showing that the way of love overturns the rules approach of parts of the Old Testament, epitomized in the thinking of the scribes and the Pharisees of Jesus' time. Some other Christians think this approach is dangerously wrong because it underestimates the value of rules for keeping people on the right track. They fear that it fails to make Christian lives distinctive and that important virtues such as justice and honesty get forgotten.

Virtue-based approaches

These two ways of approaching ethics, one based on good rules and the other based on good consequences, sometimes seem to be implacably opposed. While most people can see the usefulness of rules and the need to consider consequences in trying to decide the right thing to do in a particular situation, when each approach is applied separately, the outcomes are often different. The rule that taking innocent human life is wrong might lead us to think it would be wrong to have an abortion in any circumstances, but considering all the consequences of carrying to term and then giving birth to an unwanted child (in the case of the rape of a teenager, for example) might lead us to the opposite conclusion.

The third approach to ethics allows us to incorporate different approaches in a coherent single scheme, by making a link between right actions and good, or virtuous, people. Living well is then about working to become a better person. The aim is not to acquire the ability to think clearly about rules or consequences, and then have the strength of will to do what we believe is right. The aim is to achieve a harmony between our feelings and our actions; to think and feel; to perceive and react correctly; and to have the skills and habits to do what is right naturally, eagerly, and joyfully. Then we will act honestly, generously, and courageously because we are honest, generous, and courageous people.

Deciding the right thing to do in a particular situation will involve asking questions about what makes good a character rather than what makes good rules or good consequences. What virtues would a good person display in this situation? How can I act so as to develop these virtues in my character, display them in my behavior, and promote them in my community? Put formally, an action is right if, and only if, it is what a virtuous moral agent would characteristically do in those circumstances. A simple example of this sort of approach is the WWJD (What Would Jesus Do?) logo that some Christians use on wristbands, badges, and bookmarks.

Deciding the right thing to do in a particular situation will involve asking questions about what makes good a character rather than what makes good rules or good consequences.

Further thought is needed here about what counts as a good character. What virtues should we try to acquire? The ideas we have inherited from Aristotle answer this question by defining a virtue as a character trait (a disposition to think, feel, and react, as well as act, in certain ways) that tends toward human flourishing, that helps us to achieve an admirable, worthwhile, satisfying, and authentic life, to fulfill our idea of human life at its best.

Virtues and cultures

This suggests that there are rational and biological bases for deciding what the virtues are, which are independent of worldviews or cultures, although the traditions and values of particular communities will obviously play a part too. You could, for example, argue that because human beings are essentially social animals with young to raise, the virtues that lead to trusting, caring, peaceful, and sustained relationships will always be important if people are to flourish.

Virtues are, however, also named in language, exemplified in myths, expressed in rituals, and recorded in authoritative writings. This is as true of secular ideas about virtues as it is of religious ones. There are, for example, many stories (novels and films) and secular rituals that extol the virtue of fighting and being prepared to die for one's country.[31] Christians have a unique repository of virtues in their Scriptures, rituals, institutions, and traditions, and especially in Jesus' teaching about righteousness.

Practical wisdom

These approaches are not, at their most basic level, about judging individual actions to be right or wrong but about pursuing excellences—having an ideal in mind toward which we strive. As we have seen, according to virtue-based approaches, learning to live well is a matter of acquiring (pursuing, cultivating) the virtues and eliminating (turning away from, weeding out) the vices.

This means being able not only to identify the virtues but also to apply and use them. Aristotle thought that this involved developing what is usually translated as "practical wisdom," which is acquired more like a practical skill than a piece of information, and is learned by watching, imitating, and training. It grows with experience. Christians have the life of Jesus to follow and many examples to learn from, such as Paul applying godly virtues to particular situations. In Philippians 2, Paul tells us that we should aspire to the sort of humility that the story of Jesus reveals, and in his letter to Philemon he urges the slave owner to show generosity and mercy in his response to the return of the runaway slave.

wrestling with life's tough issues

One of the insights of Virtue Ethics is the connection between the virtues—the realization that to be virtuous is to have them all and to have the wisdom to balance them, knowing when and how much of each one is appropriate for each situation. Virtues can go wrong if they are used unwisely or inappropriately. Having the virtue of honesty, for example, involves knowing how much honesty is appropriate to a particular situation: too little honesty in one situation can become disingenuity or perfidy, while too much honesty in another situation can become insensitivity or lack of discretion. Similarly, with courage or generosity, practical wisdom picks the middle path between foolhardiness and cowardice, between profligacy and meanness.

Judging others

The actions of other Christians can then be judged not by whether they are in line with a rule or single principle, but by whether they express the virtues that the Bible holds up for us, whether they are actions that show love, justice, mercy, honesty, generosity, and humility.

Christians who see ethics in this way will look in the Bible for ways of discerning what God is like, what the story and teaching of Jesus show us about human life at its best, and what virtues God looks for in the people of his kingdom. They will take seriously the laws that God gave to his people in the Old Testament and note the way Jesus used them to identify virtues—excellences of motive and character—in the Sermon on the Mount. They will look at the way Paul applied the Christian virtues in different situations.

Christians who see ethics in this way will look in the Bible for ways of discerning what God is like, what the story and teaching of Jesus show us about human life at its best, and what virtues God looks for in the people of his kingdom.

Having identified the virtues of care, benevolence, and impartiality, they will then want to consider carefully the consequences that their actions will have, both for other people and for themselves. They will look closely at passages in the New Testament that tell us how to develop a Christian character—by listening to and walking with the Spirit of God within us, so that he can produce his fruits in our lives: "love, joy, peace, patience, kindness, goodness, faithfulness, gentleness and self-control" (Galatians 5:22–23).

Section 2

Virtue Ethics applied

An introduction to the stories

IN THIS SECTION OF THE book, you will read about seven fictional characters who each find themselves with a moral decision to make. Angela is divorced and wants to get married again; Colin is seriously considering whether or not to take his own life; Desmond has an awkward meeting coming up and wonders if, on this occasion, it would be better not to tell the truth; Charlotte is unexpectedly pregnant; Alice wants to go on a peace march but her father is against it; Timothy and Patricia receive an unexpected inheritance. These are all Christians who have consciously chosen to follow Jesus and genuinely and earnestly want to live by the teaching of the Bible. Each of them turns for help to one particular passage in the Bible, although this often leads them to other passages too.

Because the issue of same-sex relationships is a particularly contentious one in the Church at this time, it will be left to readers to think through for themselves how the Virtue Ethics approach might illuminate passages such as 1 Corinthians 6 and Romans 1.

For each character, we will see what guidance they discover from the Bible passage if they come firstly looking for rules—thinking that moral living is basically about keeping God's moral rules—and secondly thinking that moral living is basically about love, about caring equally for the well-being of everyone who will be affected, and so, in effect, looking at the consequences of their actions.

I hope that by separating out these two assumptions, which many Christians hold together in a rather unsatisfactory way, three issues will become clear: first, the difficulties and inadequacies of both approaches when they are used to interpret biblical material on their own; second, the difficulty of combining the two approaches to come to a clear view on what the Bible is teaching; and third, the potential for conflict when different Christians emphasize one approach rather than the other.

We will then explore what guidance these people find from the Bible passage if they come thinking that moral living is basically about pursuing the Christian virtues, a process which will include recognizing both the usefulness of God's laws and the need never to lose sight of love.

Interspersed between these stories will be some reflections on how the ideas of Virtue Ethics illuminate some aspect of the Bible's ethical teaching— righteousness, freedom, wisdom, love, peace, and grace. This is because Christians have mostly, down through the ages and across the traditions, not sought to find guidance in how to live from proof texts, or even proof passages. A biblical worldview is to be sought rather from the whole sweep of Scripture, with an understanding of its dynamic as well as its prescriptive nature.

My hope is that these stories and reflections can point a way out of the confusion that many Christians experience about the Bible's attitude to the moral dilemmas in which they find themselves, and that they will also provide a way of starting to resolve the conflict that so often arises among Christians about how those dilemmas should be addressed.

4

Angela considers a second marriage and looks at Matthew 5

ANGELA'S STORY

Angela is a young Christian woman living in Australia who consciously tries to live by the ethics of the Bible. At a Christian youth leaders' conference, she meets and discovers a strong attraction to an older man who shows her a lot of attention. Over the next few months, they develop a close friendship. Impressed by the work he does in the youth group at his local church, and concerned that her commitment to chastity before marriage is under some strain, she is persuaded to marry him within a year of their meeting. Over the next twelve months, she discovers that he is a cruel and violent man, that he has been implicated in the sexual abuse of children, and that she is pregnant.

Angela's husband is removed from the youth work team and leaves the church. Angela, with deep regret for what now appears to have been a bad mistake on her part, takes the advice of a Christian counselor and applies for a divorce to end the marriage. She obtains the divorce quite quickly and, because of his history, her husband is denied access to their child. Having no close family of her own in Australia, Angela moves to England with her baby daughter to start a new life.

Being a single parent in a new country turns out to be lonely and stressful, until Angela gets involved in a local church and meets Richard there—a gentle, single Christian man with a kind and supportive extended family. She and her daughter both come to love him. He then tells her he would like to marry her and adopt her daughter as his own.

ANGELA TURNS TO THE BIBLE

Angela is aware that she has not really worked out for herself what the Bible says about divorce and remarriage, so she turns to Matthew 5 for guidance, where she reads that Jesus said:

> You have heard that it was said, "Do not commit adultery." But I tell you that anyone who looks at a woman lustfully has already committed adultery with her in his heart. If your right eye causes you to sin, gouge it out and throw it away. It is better for you to lose one part of your body than for your whole body to be thrown into hell. And if your right hand causes you to sin, cut it off and throw it away. It is better for you to lose one part of your body than for your whole body to go into hell.
>
> It has been said, "Anyone who divorces his wife must give her a certificate of divorce." But I tell you that anyone who divorces his wife, except for marital unfaithfulness, causes her to become an adulteress, and anyone who marries the divorced woman commits adultery. (Matthew 5:27–32)

THREE APPROACHES TO SOLVING THE PROBLEM

LOOKING FOR RULES

Let us first imagine that Angela approaches this passage looking for a universal rule for Christians about divorce and remarriage. Reading it simply, and presuming that it applies to women divorcing men as well as men divorcing women, she will take the last sentence to mean that because her request for a divorce was not precipitated by her husband's sexual unfaithfulness, but by his cruelty and violence and the danger he might be to their daughter, she is prohibited from remarrying. Doing so would make both Richard and her guilty of adultery, which, Jesus indicates earlier in the passage, is prohibited in the law and so will lead them both to hell.

Angela is aware that she has not really worked out for herself what the Bible says about divorce and remarriage, so she turns to Matthew 5 for guidance.

Angela, however, owns some Bible commentaries[32] and, turning to them, she discovers that trying to make a universal rule from this verse is not as

wrestling with life's tough issues

straightforward as it might seem. The commentaries encourage her to think about these statements in their cultural context. Jesus is talking about men divorcing their wives, women in Jewish law at the time having limited rights to initiate divorce proceedings. To reach a universal rule, she has to presume that the rule is the same for women, even though it seems to her that, for women, physical danger is a better reason for ending a marriage than adultery.

She discovers that it is not at all clear what the phrase translated "marital unfaithfulness" ("fornication" in the King James version) means, this being a point of dispute among Jews at the time. Does it just mean sexual unfaithfulness, as people today would assume, or are there other ways of being unfaithful to one's marriage vows?

Angela then looks at Matthew 19, where some of this teaching is repeated. The context here is that some Pharisees have asked Jesus to take sides in a dispute on the question of what counts as a valid reason for a divorce. They ask him, in verse 3, "Is it lawful for a man to divorce his wife for any and every reason?"

Her commentary tells her that there was a dispute at the time between two rabbinic schools about the meaning of a verse in Deuteronomy, where the law permits a man to divorce his wife (and for her to remarry) if she "becomes displeasing to him because he finds something indecent about her" (Deuteronomy 24:1). One side took this verse to mean, if she becomes displeasing for "any and every reason" (hence the question in Matthew 19:3), while the other took it to mean, only if the man discovers she has committed adultery.

Jesus' first reply can be seen as a refusal to take sides with either of them. He points them back to the ideal of marriage—two people irreparably joined together—quoting from Genesis, "They will become one flesh" (Genesis 2:24), and adding, "What God has joined together, let man not separate" (Matthew 19:6). When the Pharisees remind him that the Jewish law permitted divorce, Jesus says that Moses allowed this law "because your hearts were hard" (Matthew 19:8), and then repeats the teaching on divorce and remarriage from Matthew 5:32.

Angela learns that, in fact, the Jewish law allowed divorce not only for "indecency" (from Deuteronomy 24:1), the meaning of which was disputed among the rabbinic schools, but also for material and emotional neglect (from Exodus 21:10–11), which most of the rabbis accepted. So, is Jesus rejecting this reason for divorce and siding with the harder interpretation based on Deuteronomy 24, or is he only saying that "any-and-every-reason" divorces are not legal?

Angela finds that when Jesus' teaching on divorce is reported in two of the other Gospels (Mark 10:11–12 and Luke 16:18), there are significant differences. Mark, writing for a Gentile readership, includes women divorcing their husbands, and both say plainly, without the addition of any exception clause, that those who divorce and remarry become adulterers.

Angela then considers Paul's teaching in 1 Corinthians 7: "To the married I give this command (not I, but the Lord): A wife must not separate from her husband. But if she does, she must remain unmarried or else be reconciled to her husband. And a husband must not divorce his wife" (vv. 10–11). Later in the same chapter, however, Paul says that if an unbeliever leaves a marriage to a Christian, "a believing man or woman is not bound in such circumstances; God has called us to live in peace" (v. 15).

What is the rule?

Angela has turned to the Bible looking for a universal rule. It is clearly not easy to deduce a coherent law for Christians from this diverse and, to us, somewhat opaque teaching. From Matthew 5:32 and 1 Corinthians 7:15, an argument can possibly be made for remarriage if the partner's adultery or desertion precipitated the divorce, but neither of these reasons applies to Angela.

The weight of the teaching taken plainly, she decides, is that Jesus prohibits the initiation of divorce proceedings by anyone in any circumstances and even more strongly condemns anyone who remarries after a divorce. This is confirmed when she learns that the Christian Church, once it had moved away from its Jewish roots, took this line and held it in a fairly consistent way until quite recently.

Angela has turned to the Bible looking for a universal rule. It is clearly not easy to deduce a coherent law for Christians from this diverse and, to us, somewhat opaque teaching.

The ambiguous or contradictory notes struck in the New Testament on this subject can, she discovers, be explained. Perhaps a later Jewish editor added the exception clause in Matthew because some of the Pharisees were arguing for divorce to be compulsory if a wife had committed adultery, and Paul was perhaps talking about something else when he said that a Christian believer is not bound to a unbelieving spouse who leaves the marriage.

Angela's conclusion

Angela concludes that until she can establish that her former husband has died, the right thing to do in this situation is to ask God to forgive her

wrestling with life's tough issues

for the mistakes of the past and then deny her strongly felt need for a loving, intimate partner, her desire to return and enjoy Richard's love, and her sense of responsibility to provide protection and care for her daughter. She must turn this offer down and bring up her daughter alone. Angela knows that many people will find this conclusion hard to understand, but she also knows that Christians are called to live distinctive lives.

LOOKING AT CONSEQUENCES

Some Christians will agree with this outcome. Others may respond by thinking that it does not seem a good resolution of the situation, that it doesn't reflect God's readiness to forgive and his concern for us to live abundant and joyful lives—that something has perhaps gone wrong here.

If Angela thinks that ethical questions should be decided not on the basis of looking for rules but on the basis of looking at consequences, she will find it hard to find any helpful guidance from Matthew 5.

If Angela thinks that ethical questions should be decided not on the basis of looking for rules but on the basis of looking at consequences, she will find it hard to find any helpful guidance from Matthew 5. It seems to say that the consequences of her marrying Richard are that both of them will become adulterers and in danger of going to hell—far more important than any consequences for anyone in this life.

Angela's conclusion

If she is going to make any sense of the consequence approach, Angela will have to put this passage out of her mind and say something like, "Ah, but in other places both Jesus and Paul tell us that all the commandments can be summed up with the rule, 'Love your neighbor as yourself' [see Luke 10:27 and Romans 13:9]. If I apply this to my situation, the consequences of my not marrying Richard are all bad—heartbreak, self-denial, and loneliness for both of us and no father for my child—while the consequences of marrying him are all good. Surely love tells me that this is the right way forward?"

Thinking a bit deeper, she may see that her going into a second marriage may make it easier for other people to enter marriage, or start divorce proceedings, without sufficient thought, but this argument seems rather removed from the intensity of her own situation.

Some Christians will agree with this outcome: God is full of mercy and wants us to live abundant lives. Others may respond that it is deeply unsatisfactory because it does not seem to take on board, at any level, what Jesus says about divorce in Matthew 5 and 19. However much you try to read into the context, Jesus did not say that in the case of divorce and remarriage love makes everything right.

LOOKING FOR VIRTUES

What happens if Angela comes to Matthew neither merely looking for universal rules nor just considering the consequences of her choices, but looking for help to develop the practical wisdom of a virtuous person, asking herself, "What sort of character is Jesus pointing his followers toward in this passage? What virtues need to be expressed in this situation?"

Angela might then notice that in this whole chapter, Jesus is considering the ethical rules laid down in the Old Testament. He commends them as good guides, but he goes on to teach that we must look beyond them to what they show us about the sort of character that fits into the kingdom of heaven. We should not, for example, simply aspire to avoid murdering anyone, but to become gentle, generous, and merciful people.

"What sort of character is Jesus pointing his followers toward in this passage? What virtues need to be expressed in this situation?"

When Jesus looks at the old rule about adultery, he tells us that it points beyond the simple prohibition of certain outward actions toward the virtue of faithfulness as an excellence to be continually pursued.

Jesus seems to be saying that the sort of faithfulness for which Christians should be aiming is deep in the character and informs not only their outward actions but also their reactions, thoughts and feelings. Angela sees that the challenge is not only to avoid unfaithful behavior but also to become faithful people. For someone who perfectly possesses the virtue of faithfulness, divorce and remarriage will not come into the picture: marriage will be joyfully exclusive and lifelong. Jesus recognizes in Matthew 19, however, that this is difficult and we all fall short of this sort of perfection.

Angela will be able to see that the hard consequences that Jesus outlines in the section on divorce can be taken in the same way as the hard consequences

wrestling with life's tough issues

outlined in the section that precedes it—not about literally gouging eyes out, cutting hands off, or condemning people to stoning (or to single parenthood), but as a picturesque emphasis on how important it is, for our physical, social, and spiritual well-being, to pursue and possess these virtues.

From a Virtue Ethics perspective, seeing that the virtue of faithfulness is involved in her decision is just a start, for virtues have to be skillfully applied: any one virtue needs to be balanced by others that are also involved. Virtues can go wrong if they are applied inappropriately. High on her agenda will be the virtues of a proper self-regard (a valuing of one's own life) and of being a responsible parent. Loving yourself is high on Jesus' agenda (Matthew 22:39), and Angela knows that she needs to find a middle ground: too much self-love can turn into the vice of selfishness, and too little self-love can turn into the vice of self-deprecation. She discovers that responsible parenting (admittedly, only for fathers) is held up as a virtue by Paul in passages such as Ephesians 6:4.

High on her agenda will be the virtues of a proper self-regard (a valuing of one's own life) and of being a responsible parent.

An ideally virtuous agent, though seeing faithfulness as the most relevant virtue here, can question the practical wisdom of remaining faithful to a man who is a danger to a child, and to a vow made with the best of intentions but inadequate knowledge. Jesus' teaching will cause Angela deep regret over the way her life has gone and an intention not to act so precipitously or foolishly again. She will carefully think through the implications of making another commitment, determining with God's help to become a more faithful person, in the hope that marriage may become more honored and respected in her community.

Angela's conclusion

Her commitment to pursuing these Christian virtues, her love for Richard, her strong feelings about her own need, and her love and responsibility for her child will lead Angela to decide that, in this situation, remarriage is the right option for her.

5

Righteousness

In the last chapter, we reflected on three different ways of approaching a passage from the Sermon on the Mount. They led us to different conclusions about the Bible's guidance for the particular situation we were considering. Christians may be divided about which of these outcomes is correct, so we now need to ask whether we can justify approaching this section of Scripture in any of these ways, independently of those results. We shall do this by looking at what Jesus teaches about the nature of righteousness and how we should go about acquiring it, mainly from Matthew 5 and Matthew 23.

Jesus' first words in the Gospel of Matthew are his reply to John the Baptist when John expresses a reluctance to baptize him: "Let it be so now; it is proper for us to do this to fulfill all righteousness" (Matthew 3:15). The opening section of the Sermon on the Mount contains the words, "Blessed are those who hunger and thirst for righteousness, for they will be filled" (Matthew 5:6). Jesus says later, "But seek first [your heavenly Father's] kingdom and

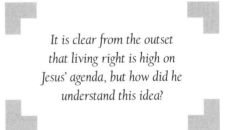

It is clear from the outset that living right is high on Jesus' agenda, but how did he understand this idea?

his righteousness" (Matthew 6:33). It is clear from the outset that living right is high on Jesus' agenda, but how did he understand this idea?

RIGHTEOUSNESS IN THE OLD TESTAMENT

In the Old Testament, we read that Abram "believed the Lord, and he credited it to him as righteousness" (Genesis 15:6), and God entered a covenant with him and his descendants. As this covenant developed under Moses, righteousness was presented as involving faithfulness to the requirements of the covenant made between God and his chosen people. God is righteous when he judges justly and when he comes as his people's deliverer, and God's people are righteous when they live the life outlined for them in the laws of Moses. The aim of these laws is that God's people should reflect the nature of their God—his holiness, justice, faithfulness, and mercy—but the prophets record for us both the people's inability to mold their lives by the laws and the judgments that resulted.

Jesus teaches his disciples what righteousness means, not in terms of the old covenant but in terms of "the kingdom of heaven."

One of the Old Testament prophets foretold that, because of this failure, there would one day be a new covenant. The laws would not be abolished but, God said, "I will put my law in their minds and write it on their hearts. . . . No longer will a man teach his neighbor, or a man his brother, saying, 'Know the Lord,' because they will all know me" (Jeremiah 31:33–34).

JESUS ON RIGHTEOUSNESS

In the Sermon on the Mount (Matthew 5–7), which is most probably a compilation of Jesus' ethical teaching, Jesus teaches his disciples what righteousness means, not in terms of the old covenant but in terms of "the kingdom of heaven," because Jesus has come to inaugurate a new way of living under God's rule.

We can ask whether any of the approaches we have been considering seem to fit this teaching better than the others. Is Jesus talking about simply acting out of love for everyone? How important are rules here? Are we meant to be identifying and conforming to prohibitions and obligations, or is the main emphasis on the aspiration to develop a distinctive character?

Jesus begins his sermon by affirming his Galilean audience (who would have been predominantly the ordinary farmers, shepherds, and fisherfolk). He does this by describing the character of those most likely to end up in God's kingdom—not the self-assured, secure, ambitious, and powerful, but the humble, struggling, and meek, those who have the right values and care about living right, those who are merciful, engaged in making peace and persecuted by their enemies.

He then affirms the ethical teaching of the Old Testament: "Do not think that I have come to abolish the Law or the Prophets; I have not come to abolish them but to fulfill them. . . . Whoever practices and teaches these commands will be called great in the kingdom of heaven" (Matthew 5:17, 19).

Jesus goes on to voice what will become quite a theme in Matthew's Gospel—criticism of some of the groups within the Judaism of his time who thought themselves the most righteous: "Unless your righteousness surpasses that of the Pharisees and the teachers of the law, you will certainly not enter the kingdom of heaven" (v. 20). In the rest of Matthew 5, Jesus develops this idea by taking one particular Old Testament law after another and applying it in a different way from the Pharisees, with some startlingly picturesque language.

Let us first note that Jesus is not saying that love, in the sense of concern for other people's happiness, is the only virtue Christians need to live righteous lives. If loving God with all our heart and soul and strength and mind, and loving our neighbor as ourselves (Luke 10:27) summarizes the law, it must mean more than that, because Jesus tells his listeners that faithfulness, self-control, and honesty are important and that pursuing these virtues does not always lead directly to the happiest outcomes for everyone.

There are, however, two other ways in which Jesus' teaching about the old Jewish law can be taken. It can be seen as a tightening up of the prohibitions and obligations that the Pharisees had applied only to outward behavior, deciding to relax and limit them when the law seemed too difficult. Jesus goes into more detail about this in Matthew 23, which we will look at later.

Under this interpretation, Jesus was saying that the rules applied in a much wider range of situations than the Pharisees had imagined: they applied not only to our acts but also to our speech, our thoughts and feelings, and our motivations. The Pharisees had been making it all too easy. Not only was adultery prohibited, but lustful looks and divorce were prohibited too (Matthew 5:27–28). Not only was there an obligation to perform righteous acts, righteous motivation was also required (6:1). This would lead us to see Jesus' teaching as closest to contemporary "rules" approaches.

In a third way of understanding his teaching about how to use the law to achieve righteousness, Jesus can be seen exhorting his followers to move on from the idea of rules as the only way of making judgments about people's behavior—to look behind the too-literal interpretation of these old laws as absolute rules about external behavior, and to see them rather as an exhortation to pursue excellence, even perfection, in our character.

Seen from this perspective, Jesus was exhorting his followers to pursue the virtues of gentleness, self-control, faithfulness, honesty, and love—not just to act gently, faithfully, and honestly, but to be gentle, faithful, and honest people. As he says in Matthew 7, "A good tree cannot bear bad fruit, and a bad tree cannot bear good fruit" (v. 18). Chapter 5 ends with the challenge, "Be perfect, therefore, as your heavenly Father is perfect" (Matthew 5:48)—perfect not only in obedient actions, but in all the virtues that God himself possesses.

Matthew 23

If we move on to Matthew 23, where Jesus goes into more detail about what is wrong about the ethics of the Pharisees, it becomes clearer whether Jesus was, in the Sermon on the Mount, hardening up the rules or pointing us beyond them. Chapter 23 again begins with Jesus showing a high regard for the law: "The teachers of the law and the Pharisees sit in Moses' seat. So you must obey them and do everything they tell you" (vv. 2–3a). Yet he immediately goes on to criticize how these groups of Jewish leaders were applying the law. "But do not do what they do, for they do not practice what they preach" (v. 3b).

> *Jesus was exhorting his followers to pursue the virtues of gentleness, self-control, faithfulness, honesty, and love—not just to act gently, faithfully, and honestly, but to be gentle, faithful, and honest people.*

Jesus accuses the Pharisees of having failed to penetrate the meaning, the intention behind the laws of Moses. The Pharisees applied them in a wooden, legalistic way, as rules against certain carefully defined categories of external behavior, rather than seeing behind them to the more important matters of "justice, mercy and faithfulness" (v. 23).

Jesus' teaching on how to use the Sabbath law confirms this. In Matthew 12, he is accused of allowing his disciples to break the law of Sabbath observance—which, technically, he had done by letting them pick corn and eat it as they walked through the fields. Jesus tells his accusers, "If you had known what these words mean, 'I desire mercy, not sacrifice,' you would not have condemned the innocent" (v. 7). Faced with a disabled man, the religious leaders then ask Jesus if it is lawful to heal on the Sabbath. He replies, "It is lawful to do good on the Sabbath," and heals the man (vv. 12–13).

Back in Matthew 23, Jesus strongly criticizes the scribes and Pharisees for supposing that they could use the law to win praise from God, or feel self-righteous and complacent about their own behavior, while at the same time judging others and putting unbearable burdens on them. They had distorted the real meaning of the law by making rules about minor issues,

wrestling with life's tough issues

such as which words could be used in oaths, tithing herbs and spices, and washing cups and plates, while neglecting the development of a God-like character. Jesus calls it, in typically picturesque language, straining out a gnat and swallowing a camel (v. 24).

Thus Jesus reveals that the real meaning of the law is as an inspiration in the pursuit of righteousness—right living—which, for God's people, involves reflecting the character of God in their lives. Paul explains that what the law could not do, God achieved for us in Jesus. Our relationship is restored through his death for us on the cross, and our growth in holiness is enabled by the gift of his Spirit as he lives and produces his fruit in us (Galatians 3:21–25; 5:16–26).

They had distorted the real meaning of the law by making rules about minor issues, such as which words could be used in oaths, tithing herbs and spices, and washing cups and plates, while neglecting the development of a God-like character.

When Jesus speaks in the Sermon on the Mount of dire consequences—of being "in danger of the fire of hell" (Matthew 5:22), of being "thrown into prison" (v. 25), and of your body going into hell (v. 30)—he is not, then, speaking of punishments for breaking rules but warning us of the danger of supposing that we are part of God's kingdom when our characters are radically incompatible with its values.

The intention of the law

Righteousness, for Jesus, thus seems to be more than outward obedience, and our pursuit of righteousness more than trying to keep a set of rules. This was the very mistake that the Pharisees were making. The humble, struggling, and merciful, those who love peace and righteousness, are welcome in the kingdom and are called not to keep kingdom rules but to become kingdom people. This was, Jesus explains, the intention of the law.

The old laws—do not murder, do not commit adultery, do not break your oath, eye for eye and tooth for tooth, love your neighbor and hate your enemy—were not meant to be turned into rigid and absolute rules that gave some people the option of self-righteousness and burdened others. They were meant to hold out, as ideals to pursue, the virtues of self-control, gentleness, amiability, conciliation, faithfulness, simplicity, honesty, generosity, inclusiveness, and love. Living this way may, in the short term, lead to persecution, but will also lead us to achieve a life that is blessed by God. "I have come," Jesus said, "that they may have life, and have it to the full" (John 10:10).

Approaching the Bible from a Virtue Ethics perspective thus helps us to find, in Jesus' teaching on righteousness, continuity with the Old Testament and cohesive and practical guidance on how to live well.

6

Colin thinks about taking his own life and looks at Galatians 5

Colin's story

Colin is 79. He retired from his profession as a pharmacist at 65, and his wife died of cancer shortly afterward. Since then, he has lived on his own, the local church becoming his main source of both friendship and service. Colin has two married sons who have moved away from the area and very rarely contact him. He hardly knows his five grandchildren. A few months ago, Colin's only remaining sibling and the friend from church with whom he spent the most time both died.

Colin suffers from arthritis. After the two funerals, when just getting around seemed to become more painful and difficult, his vicar suggested that he give up his place on the church council, his role on the welcome team, and the volunteer work he had been doing at the local shelter for the homeless.

When Colin consulted his doctor, she told him that she could prescribe drugs that would help him with the pain and stiffness, and that he should be able to live a fairly active life for a few more years. Eventually, though, he would have to use a wheelchair and would need full-time nursing care, possibly for quite a number of years.

The doctor's prognosis has led Colin to feel that his life has no value now, to himself or to anyone else. As a Christian, he feels at peace about dying but is simply tired of his lonely, painfully restricted life, and the prospect of losing his independence and his dignity fills him with dread.

Colin has considerable savings and owns a large house. He has given quite a lot of thought to what will happen to these assets when he dies. Feelings of resentment at his sons' neglect have grown into hostility and for some time he has been considering changing his will.

Other thoughts have also been going around in Colin's head. With his pharmaceutical knowledge, he realizes that he could quite easily accumulate sufficient prescription drugs to kill himself gently and painlessly. If he does this before he needs full-time nursing care, he reflects, he can avoid the dependency he dreads and do some good by leaving his savings and the proceeds from the sale of his house to one of the Christian charities he supports.

Colin has a natural revulsion toward the act of suicide but knows that Christians are called to give their lives in the service of others and wants to know whether this might be the right response to his present situation.

Then Colin hears that the funding is being withdrawn for the local shelter for the homeless, which his church supports, and it will have to shut down unless it can find a large sum of money within the next year. He has a natural revulsion toward the act of suicide but knows that Christians are called to give their lives in the service of others and wants to know whether this might be the right response to his present situation.

COLIN TURNS TO THE BIBLE

Colin looks for some teaching on suicide in the Bible, but finds that the few stories of people taking their own lives are told without much moral comment (see Judges 16:30, 1 Samuel 31:4–5, 2 Samuel 17:23, 1 Kings 16:18, and Matthew 27:5). He knows that one of the Ten Commandments talks about not taking human life (Exodus 20:13), but also that this is about murder— unlawful killing—rather than any taking of life; legitimate war and criminal execution, for example, were clearly not included. So can suicide be the right response to some situations for a Christian? Colin comes across Galatians 5 and reads it, looking for help.

It is for freedom that Christ has set us free. Stand firm, then, and do not let yourselves be burdened again by a yoke of slavery. . . . You who are trying to be justified by law have been alienated from Christ; you have fallen away from grace. But by faith we eagerly await through the Spirit the righteousness for which we hope. For in Christ Jesus neither circumcision nor uncircumcision has any value. The only thing that counts is faith expressing itself through love. . . .

wrestling with life's tough issues

You, my brothers, were called to be free. But do not use your freedom to indulge the sinful nature; rather, serve one another in love. The entire law is summed up in a single command: "Love your neighbor as yourself." If you keep on biting and devouring each other, watch out or you will be destroyed by each other.

So I say, live by the Spirit, and you will not gratify the desires of the sinful nature. For the sinful nature desires what is contrary to the Spirit, and the Spirit what is contrary to the sinful nature. They are in conflict with each other, so that you do not do what you want. But if you are led by the Spirit, you are not under law.

The acts of the sinful nature are obvious: sexual immorality, impurity and debauchery; idolatry and witchcraft; hatred, discord, jealousy, fits of rage, selfish ambition, dissensions, factions and envy; drunkenness, orgies, and the like. I warn you, as I did before, that those who live like this will not inherit the kingdom of God.

But the fruit of the Spirit is love, joy, peace, patience, kindness, goodness, faithfulness, gentleness and self-control. Against such things there is no law. Those who belong to Christ Jesus have crucified the sinful nature with its passions and desires. Since we live by the Spirit, let us keep in step with the Spirit. (Galatians 5:1, 4–6, 13–25)

THREE APPROACHES TO SOLVING THE PROBLEM

LOOKING FOR RULES

If Colin is looking in the Bible for rules that relate to his present dilemma, he will not find anything very helpful in this passage from Galatians. The only rule he can find here is "Love your neighbor as yourself," which Paul says sums up the entire law. If Colin loves his own life, he will want to hold on to it, and if he loves the homeless as much as he loves himself, it could be argued that he would want to give up his life for their sake.

The list of actions that Paul says come from the sinful nature may be considered as a list of prohibitions, and Colin may see idolatry or selfish ambition in his desire to preserve his own life in this situation.

Exploring further, however, Colin discovers that in the fourth century, a Christian bishop (Augustine of Hippo, 353–430) decided that suicide was murder so it was covered by the sixth commandment. The Christian Church followed him in this idea for centuries, teaching that suicide was not permitted behavior for Christians and withholding Christian burial from people who had taken their own lives.

Colin lives in Britain, where suicide was considered a crime until 1961.[33] Colin found that, while many Christian churches still officially say that suicide is technically wrong on the grounds that only God has the right to give and take life, in individual situations people are rarely blamed or criticized.

In the United States suicide was historically considered under common law to be a crime, punishable by the forfeiture of the property of the offender or ignominious burial. Under modern law, however, suicide is no longer a crime. Some states still classify suicide as a criminal act, but prosecution is rare.

Colin's conclusion

If Colin were looking in the Bible for rules about suicide, he would probably, in view of these discoveries, decide that it would not be the right course of action for him to take, even if he were not certain that the Church's interpretation of Exodus 20:13 was the interpretation understood at the time the law was given, or that it was necessarily the only legitimate way of looking at it today. Some Christians will agree that this is the best decision for Colin.

LOOKING AT CONSEQUENCES

Let us imagine, however, that after hearing a sermon on Paul's attitude to the law, Colin goes back to the passage again. He now wonders if Augustine's pronouncement about suicide in the fourth century might be an example of returning to the slavery of law, from which Christ has freed us.

If Colin were looking in the Bible for rules about suicide, he would probably, in view of these discoveries, decide that it would not be the right course of action for him to take.

When he reads that Christ has set us free from the law—that if we are "led by the Spirit" we are not "under law"—Colin takes Paul to mean that we no longer have to live by rules and should stand firm against being entangled by them again. "The only thing that counts," Paul says, "is faith expressing itself through love." "Love your neighbor as yourself" sums up the entire law.

wrestling with life's tough issues

Two courses of action

If acting with love means acting in a way that produces the best outcomes and the least harm for everyone affected, then, Colin argues to himself, there must be situations in which taking one's own life would be the right thing to do. He can find out if his situation is one of these by comparing the consequences of both possible courses of action.

If Colin takes his own life now, the shelter for the homeless will get the funding it needs, and many of the most vulnerable people in the community will be shown Christian love and will even have an opportunity to hear the gospel. Colin feels a burden of care for the people he met at the shelter while he worked there and counts this as a very good outcome—an example of "serving one another in love."

His sons and their families will not, in this case, get the inheritance they are expecting, but they are both quite well off so the harm there will be slight. They will have to face the loss of their father one day, and he doesn't think they will be too distressed about his death now rather than after a long and awkward illness. In fact, they may be quite relieved. By depriving them of his company, he will not be depriving them of anything that is of value to them, or they would have kept in touch. It might, in the long term, do them some good to feel rebuked for their neglect, and there is no one else close enough to him to be more than marginally affected by his death.

> If acting with love means acting in a way that produces the best outcomes and the least harm for everyone affected, then, Colin argues to himself, there must be situations in which taking one's own life would be the right thing to do.

If Colin decides not to kill himself at this point in his life, he can still change his will so his sons don't get the money they don't need or, in his opinion, deserve. He can also give some money to the shelter now—though not enough to save it from closing because, if he is not to be a financial burden to others, he will need to make sure he has enough to pay for the sort of prolonged nursing care his illness will require, and he will also need to keep his house to live in for the time being.

Colin's conclusion

Colin feels that he no longer contributes anything of value to anyone, not to his family, his church, or his local community. No one will miss him in a deep or distressing way when he goes, and he will in the future be an increasing burden on them all. Far better that he should leave this life now and, in going, do some good.

Some Christians may agree with the result of this way of thinking. Others may feel that by concentrating only on the consequences of his action for other people, Colin has missed a great deal about the morality of suicide and the meaning of love. To include these factors in his thinking, Colin does not have to return to the idea of living by rules, however.

LOOKING FOR VIRTUES

Approaching the Galatians passage again, looking for virtues to pursue, Colin sees that Paul does indeed think that Christians are free from the yoke of having to keep universal rules. Love is the basis for Christian ethics, but Paul fills out the idea of Christian love with a list of other virtues. Living with Christian love is, it seems, a great deal more than calculating consequences impartially, for there are some virtues here that relate to our behavior toward others and some that we might call "self-regarding" virtues. Joy, peace, and patience, for example, to some extent reflect how we feel about our own rather than other people's lives. It is also not appropriate to think of everyone affected as being equal in our calculations because there are some virtues that relate to special relationships: responsibility for our children or the people we work with may carry more weight in our calculations, for instance, than our responsibility for strangers.

Colin now begins to see that suicide is, in many ways, a very personal action. It does have profound effects on other people who witness or hear about it, but it also expresses how we evaluate our own life in particular and human life in general. How we die, quite as much as how we live, can reveal our character, our beliefs, and our values.

Does Colin have the grace to see his life as a gift from God—something to cherish and protect? Can he trust God for the spiritual gifts of joy and peace? Can he pursue the virtues of patience and contentment? Can he witness to his community that human life has a value, a sort of sacredness, even when health and strength are gone?

Colin looks at his motives

When he gives attention to the virtues that Paul specifically mentions in this passage, Colin begins to think about his motives. We may be free from law, but Paul says that we should not use our freedom to indulge the sinful nature.

Colin finds that he can detect three things lurking behind his admirable desire to do good to the homeless. First, there is the resentment he harbors about his sons' neglect of him, and his desire to let them know how they have hurt him. He decides that "revenge" is perhaps too strong a word, but he can detect some malice there rather than the kindness that Paul is commending.

Second, Colin notices that among the vices in Paul's list are discord and dissension. He begins to wonder if the discord in his family might, to some extent, be his fault. Has he been faithful in keeping in touch with his sons and their families? Has he shared his news and feelings with them? Has he ever tried to make himself useful to them or to develop a relationship with his grandchildren? He begins to see the possibility of new projects for his remaining active years.

> *Colin finds himself being challenged by these thoughts to think again about the value of his life. Was it precipitous and presumptuous of him to make the judgment that his life was worthless?*

Third, there is the fear of losing his independence and dignity. Could this be construed as cowardice in the face of a new challenge? Has a healthy desire for self-determination become an unhealthy fear of losing control, of being the recipient of other people's generosity? Does he perhaps have a problem with pride or with trust?

He comes to see that there is a natural pattern to human life. We begin in total dependence on others. We grow out of this and into a time when others (sometimes both our children and our parents) are dependent on us. We become free of dependents and then fulfill the circle by ourselves becoming dependent on others again. Perhaps, Colin considers, there are useful roles to play, joys to be discovered, and lessons that God has to teach us in each of these stages of life.

Some new projects

Colin finds himself being challenged by these thoughts to think again about the value of his life. Was it precipitous and presumptuous of him to make the judgment that his life was worthless? Was it perhaps the product of a period of depression after the death of his sister and his friend? There are, in fact, already several projects occurring to him that could give his life new meaning and value. He can have a go at reconstructing his family life, trying, even if it is rather late in the day, to be a father and grandfather in some pale reflection of God's kind fathering of him.

He notices Paul's phrase, "By faith we eagerly await through the Spirit the righteousness for which we hope" (Galatians 5:5). This search for righteousness, this pursuit of Christian virtues, is something that can go on until the day he dies, regardless of—perhaps even inspired and energized by—the decline and decrepitude of his body. Even in a nursing home he can be "Christ in the world" to those around him, witnessing to them of faith and hope and love.

All these positive thoughts, which Colin can already feel lifting his depression, must of course be balanced against the good that could be done in keeping the shelter for the homeless open, but Colin can give what he can and perhaps do some fund-raising from home, and the sum needed may be reached without the sacrifice of several years of his life.

Colin's conclusion

Colin can see that there might be situations in which giving up one's life is the right thing for a Christian to do, where it would reflect the Christian virtues—if, for example, other lives might be saved—but after studying Galatians 5, he decides that committing suicide is not one of them.

7

Freedom

When someone faces a specific ethical dilemma, such as the one in the previous chapter, they can approach Galatians 5 in one of a number of ways. They can look for rules to keep, consequences to optimize, or virtues to pursue—and the resulting decisions about the right action to take will turn out to be different. Our own ethical wisdom may lead us to favor one of these decisions over the others, but we now need to ask whether we can independently justify coming to the passage using one of those approaches rather than the others.

We shall do this by looking at Galatians 5 in the context of the whole letter and, in particular, its central theme of freedom. In Galatians 3:28, Paul remarks on some of the distinctions between people in the society of his day, one of these being that some people lived in slavery and others were free. This was a powerful example for both the writer and the recipients of this letter.

PAUL'S GOSPEL OF GRACE

It appears that there was a dispute in the churches of Galatia between two groups of Christian leaders. One group was teaching that people could only find justification (being counted as righteous before God) by having faith in what Jesus had done for them on the cross. This was the gospel of grace that Paul himself taught. The other group argued that all those who accepted Jesus as Lord and Savior, including Gentile converts, had to be circumcised and keep the laws of Moses. Paul described the latter group as being like those who, having been set free, voluntarily put themselves back into slavery. "You foolish Galatians!" he writes. "Who has bewitched you? . . . After beginning with the Spirit, are you now trying to attain your goal by human effort? . . . Does God give you his Spirit and work miracles among you because you observe the law, or because you believe what you heard?" (3:1, 3, 5). Paul takes his readers back to Abraham to point out that long before the law was given to Moses, Abraham "believed God, and it was credited to him as righteousness" (v. 6).

Paul's attitude to the law shows a remarkable consistency with that of Jesus. For Paul, the law is useful "to lead us to Christ that we might be justified by faith" (v. 24). It is not opposed to the promises of God (v. 21), but it was temporary (v. 19); it could not impart life (v. 21). Like Jesus, Paul also warns against the way in which the Pharisees had misinterpreted and misused the law: "Now that faith has come, we are no longer under the supervision of the law" (v. 25). We are no longer slaves to the law, and God has sent his Spirit into our hearts to witness to this fact. The Spirit "calls out, 'Abba, Father.' So you are no longer a slave, but a son" (4:6–7).

Paul continues with a long allegory about Abraham's two sons, one the son of a slave woman (Hagar) and the other the son of a free woman (Sarah). The covenant made on Mount Sinai, where the law was given, represents the woman who bears children to be slaves, but as Christians we are not the children of this woman. "The Jerusalem that is above is free, and she is our mother" (4:26).

Freedom from the law

This is the background to Paul's earnest plea: "It is for freedom that Christ has set us free. Stand firm, then, and do not let yourselves be burdened again by a yoke of slavery" (5:1). Paul has now moved his thoughts about freedom from the area of justification (being counted as righteous) to the area of sanctification (being made righteous): in verse 6 he says, "The only thing that counts is faith expressing itself through love," and in verse 13 he says, "You, my brothers, were called to be free. But do not use your freedom to indulge the sinful nature; rather, serve one another in love." By linking freedom with "the sinful nature" and with loving service, Paul shows that he is not talking only about freedom from ritual or ceremonial laws.

When someone faces a specific ethical dilemma, . . . they can approach Galatians 5 in one of a number of ways . . . the resulting decisions about the right action to take will turn out to be different.

The fact that Paul is firmly in the area of ethical living and still using the terminology of freedom from the law is confirmed in verse 14, where

wrestling with life's tough issues

he says, "The entire law is summed up in a single command: 'Love your neighbor as yourself.'"

Christians are free from having to keep the law in order to be justified before God, because it is by grace, through faith, that people are justified. They are also free from having to keep the law in order to be sanctified—to start living as befits God's children—because, as Paul will go on to explain, it is the Spirit's work to produce his fruit in our lives.

The Spirit's fruit

Paul tells the Galatian churches that knowing how to live right—how to make the right ethical decisions—will no longer be a matter of looking up the rules and obeying them but of being led by the Spirit (5:18). It will be a matter of allowing God's Spirit to produce his fruit in us (vv. 22–23). We are no longer to strive to keep rules about outward behavior; we are to strive to develop the Christian virtues in our inner character.

The question we have to ask now is what Paul means when he says, "The entire law is summed up in a single command: 'Love your neighbor as yourself'" (v. 14). Does this mean that we should let our actions be guided by an impartial concern about how they affect others, or is there more to Christian love than this?

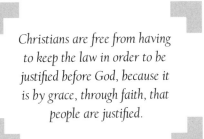

Christians are free from having to keep the law in order to be justified before God, because it is by grace, through faith, that people are justified.

Paul begins to outline the ethical task of the Christian by listing "the acts of the sinful nature" that should be avoided. These are not actions that result primarily from an inability to identify the right rules and obey them, or from an inability to calculate the best outcomes and care enough to implement them. These are actions that come from vices embedded in our natures, vices that are radically incompatible with life in God's kingdom.

What God's Spirit will achieve, if we give him the space, is neither the will to obey rules nor the ability to calculate consequences. God's Spirit will grow the Christian virtues in our character. These can be summed up by the idea of Christian love, but they are wider than impartial benevolence, for some of them are not primarily about how we relate to other people but about how we experience and value our own lives, and some of them point us to responsibilities to people with whom we have a special relationship.

The ethical task that Paul is commending to the Christians in the Galatian churches is to free themselves from the constraints of the law, from the whole way of looking at ethical living as a system of rules with rewards and punishments. We are not, however, to use this sense of freedom to indulge the traits in our characters, the vices, that are incompatible with the kingdom of which we are now part. These vices are to be stamped on or pulled up like unwelcome weeds in a garden. Rather, we are to be open to the Spirit—to "live by the Spirit" (5:16), to be "led by the Spirit" (v. 18), to "keep in step with the Spirit" (v. 25)—so that he can develop these virtues in us. Paul goes on with the horticultural analogy: it is like watering, feeding, and pruning the plants that we want to flourish, to flower, and to fruit.

What God's Spirit will achieve, if we give him the space, is neither the will to obey rules nor the ability to calculate consequences. God's Spirit will grow the Christian virtues in our character.

In Galatians 6:15, Paul sums up his arguments by saying that the old rules about outward behavior, epitomized by those relating to circumcision, mean nothing: they have no direct part to play in the justification or the sanctification of God's people now that Christ has come.

A new creation

This is the freedom that Christ has won for us. What counts now is the Spirit's new creation in the character of the believer. Our part is not to be tempted back into living by rules or to aim just at an impartial benevolence, but to nurture all the virtues of Christian love in ourselves and in other people. Paul blesses with peace and mercy all those who follow this new rule.

Paul sums up his view of freedom in 2 Corinthians 3:17–18 in a way that is, from a Virtue Ethics perspective, clear and practical. He says, "Now the Lord is the Spirit, and where the Spirit of the Lord is, there is freedom. And we, who with unveiled faces all reflect the Lord's glory, are being transformed into his likeness with ever-increasing glory, which comes from the Lord, who is the Spirit."

8

Desmond wonders about telling the truth and looks at Ephesians 4 and 5

DESMOND'S STORY

Desmond is the pastor of a group of small town churches. Alice and Terry, who have been running a store in one of the towns for almost a year, come to ask for baptism for their new baby. Desmond suggests that they start coming to church and that they have a series of meetings so that he can run through with them the basics of the Christian faith and the sort of commitment that has to be made in the baptism service.

The meetings go very well. Alice seems to have a dormant faith that is slowly coming alive. Terry seems to have a more recent Christian background and to be enthusiastic about becoming more involved in the life of the church.

On the morning of the day that has been scheduled for their last meeting, another woman from the town comes to see Desmond in some distress. She has seen the couple in church with their baby and thinks he ought to know that Terry is having an affair with her best friend and selling pornographic videos to special customers at the store. She doesn't know if Alice is aware of either of these activities.

That afternoon, Alice runs over to Desmond on the main street to say that she has been calling around and the date of next month's family service would be ideal for the baptism. Desmond hesitates and then prevaricates, and Alice notices a change in his attitude. "You were happy enough last week," she accuses, and then asks, "Has anything happened to make you change your mind?" Desmond says, "We'll talk about it tonight."

Desmond turns to the Bible

Desmond returns to the church angry and uncertain what to do, especially if Alice asks him the same question directly when they meet that evening. The truth is that, yes, something has happened, but he's not sure if it might be better, for this evening at least, not to be honest about it. He knows that Paul deals with the subject of honesty in Ephesians 4 and 5 and turns to the passage.

> It was [Christ] who gave some to be apostles, some to be prophets, some to be evangelists, and some to be pastors and teachers, to prepare God's people for works of service, so that the body of Christ may be built up until we all reach unity in the faith and in the knowledge of the Son of God and become mature, attaining to the whole measure of the fullness of Christ.
>
> Then we will no longer be infants, tossed back and forth by the waves, and blown here and there by every wind of teaching and by the cunning and craftiness of men in their deceitful scheming. Instead, speaking the truth in love, we will in all things grow up into him who is the Head, that is, Christ. . . .
>
> You were taught, with regard to your former way of life, to put off your old self, which is being corrupted by its deceitful desires; to be made new in the attitude of your minds; and to put on the new self, created to be like God in true righteousness and holiness.
>
> Therefore each of you must put off falsehood and speak truthfully to his neighbor, for we are all members of one body. 'In your anger do not sin': Do not let the sun go down while you are still angry, and do not give the devil a foothold. . . .
>
> Do not let any unwholesome talk come out of your mouths, but only what is helpful for building others up according to their needs, that it may benefit those who listen. And do not grieve the Holy Spirit of God, with whom you were sealed for the day of redemption. Get rid of all bitterness, rage and anger, brawling and slander, along with every form of malice. Be kind and compassionate to one another, forgiving each other, just as in Christ God forgave you.
>
> Be imitators of God, therefore, as dearly loved children and live a life of love, just as Christ loved us and gave himself up for us as a fragrant offering and sacrifice to God. . . .
>
> For you were once darkness, but now you are light in the Lord. Live as children of light (for the fruit of the light consists in all goodness, righteousness and truth) and find out what pleases the Lord. Have nothing to do with the fruitless deeds of darkness, but rather expose them. For it is shameful even to mention what the disobedient do in secret. . . .

wrestling with life's tough issues

Be very careful, then, how you live—not as unwise but as wise, making the most of every opportunity, because the days are evil. Therefore do not be foolish, but understand what the Lord's will is. (Ephesians 4:11–15, 22–27, 29–5:2, 8–12, 15–17)

THREE APPROACHES TO SOLVING THE PROBLEM

LOOKING FOR RULES

Desmond has known since he was about four that lying is wrong. Admittedly, he has found out since that the Ten Commandments only deal directly with one particular aspect of honesty—giving false testimony against a neighbor (Exodus 20:16)—and that when Jesus says, "Simply let your 'Yes' be 'Yes,' and your 'No,' 'No'" (Matthew 5:37), it is in the context of not using oaths to back up our assertions. The Christian Church, however, has consistently taught that Christians are prohibited from all aspects of dishonest behavior—lying, slander, deception, duplicity, insincerity, breaking promises, cheating, pretension, hypocrisy, fraud, perfidy, stealing, and so on.

If Desmond is looking for universal rules, Paul's direct command that "each of you must put off falsehood and speak truthfully to his neighbor" seems inescapable.

If Desmond is looking for universal rules, Paul's direct command that "each of you must put off falsehood and speak truthfully to his neighbor" seems inescapable. Is there, in fact, any rule that is more universally recognized and easy to justify? Without an underlying presumption that people speak the truth, any kind of social life would be impossible.

Several other phrases in the passage underline the importance of always telling the truth. Paul says that "speaking the truth in love" is the way to grow up into Christ and avoid being "blown here and there . . . by the cunning and craftiness of men in their deceitful scheming." Paul speaks of "living as children of light" because he says that "the fruit of the light consists in all goodness, righteousness and truth."

Desmond has always felt that this idea of "living in the light" means that all forms of dishonest behavior are prohibited for him, and the passage seems to suggest that he should also be prepared to expose "the fruitless deeds of darkness."

Trying to apply the rule

Desmond's problem now is in working out how to apply the rule of always telling the truth in this particular situation, while at the same time being careful to control his anger and act out of love, not malice, so that what he says "benefits those who listen." Desmond decides that if a direct question is asked, he can't hide what has happened from Alice and Terry. He will have to tell them who has come to him and what she said, and take it from there. Anything else will begin to entangle him in deception.

He feels that he must expose the truth about Terry's life, especially to Alice, if she doesn't already know it. He must also share honestly with them what he thinks the implications are for the baptism of their baby. He will need to point out to Terry that to make public statements in church about renouncing sin, without any intention of changing his life, would be plainly dishonest and something that he, Desmond, could not knowingly allow to happen in his church.

Speaking the truth, he notices, must always be done "in love," so his care about the well-being of everyone involved must be his guide.

The thought passes through his mind that the information he has been given may not be correct, but his own private judgment of Terry confirms to him that it is, and his anger at being deceived and manipulated by this man makes him want to confront Terry immediately—to get it sorted out before the sun goes down.

Desmond sees from the Ephesians passage that his role as a pastor is to build up the body of Christ "until we all reach unity in the faith." If Terry is seen to be deceiving him and is allowed to continue to deceive others, this will put the unity of the church community in danger. If Alice and Terry are serious about becoming part of the church, then the way they are behaving and the dishonesty in their relationship with him needs to be confronted.

Desmond's conclusion

The "old self" that the passage tells him to "put off" would not have had any scruples about lying in this situation, but, as a Christian, he must judge this to be the easy way out and choose the harder path. The way ahead may be stormy, but it is more important that the truth is told, that Desmond is not seen to be involved in any kind of deception, and that Terry is not allowed

wrestling with life's tough issues

to make a mockery of the church and its sacraments. Any talk of a baptism must be deferred until all this is sorted out.

LOOKING AT CONSEQUENCES

If, however, Desmond believes that living by rules might be a bit too simple of an approach to right living, and that he should rather calculate the consequences of his actions in order to decide how to proceed, his attention will be drawn to Paul's emphasis on maturity and on being "made new in the attitude of your minds." Speaking the truth, he notices, must always be done "in love," so his care about the well-being of everyone involved must be his guide. He must concentrate on building others up "according to their needs." He must be kind and compassionate. Living a life of love is, he discovers, an important part of being a child of light.

Guessing the consequences of answering Alice's question truthfully, though, is far from easy. Until he has more facts, he doesn't know what the outcome will be if he confronts the couple with the information he received in town that afternoon. Is it true?

Does Alice know how Terry has been behaving? If he is sure that the answer to both of these questions is yes, then telling the truth could have good long-term outcomes for the church, but if he is thinking in terms of personal happiness, it will almost certainly have bad short-term effects on Alice and Terry and their relationship with him, the church, and the town. Perhaps, if the situation is handled very carefully, a relatively good outcome could eventually be reached. If, however, the answer to either of the questions is no, then the outcome would be disastrous in every respect, risking serious damage to a number of relationships and the reputation of the church.

Desmond's conclusion

Desmond does not know what to do, so he decides that the best way forward is to prevaricate, see how the evening goes, play it by ear, and defer any decision about what is to be done until he has more information.

LOOKING FOR VIRTUES

Some Christians might think that approaching the passage from Ephesians looking for rules has led to an underestimation of Paul's ideas about the radical freedom of Christians in their ethical living, and caused Desmond to put too little emphasis on love, mission, and the reputation of the gospel—three things about which Paul was passionate. Looking merely at consequences, however, has meant that Desmond is left not knowing what to do, and some may feel that he has not really considered the relevance and importance of the virtue of honesty to this situation.

If Desmond comes to these Scriptures with the idea that Paul is not laying down universal rules about how to live as a Christian, but describing and exhorting Christians to pursue appropriate virtues, his thoughts about how to behave that evening will lead him to an altogether richer and clearer answer.

He knows, as Paul is pressing home here, that honesty—both in terms of a commitment to truth and of a transparency of life—is an important virtue to possess and the key factor in this situation, but he also knows that to possess a virtue involves more than keeping a rule. It involves having the wisdom to use it appropriately. He knows that any virtue has to be balanced with others and that underlying motives and character are as important as outward behavior.

Desmond notices first the exhortation to be wise: "Be very careful, then, how you live—not as unwise but as wise, making the most of every opportunity, because the days are evil. Therefore do not be foolish, but understand what the Lord's will is" (5:15-17). He has an opportunity to bring a new family into the church community, and this needs special wisdom because "the days are evil": the situation has been complicated either by immorality and deception or by slander.

Desmond knows that having the virtue of honesty involves a deep concern for the truth, so it is most important that the true situation is discovered and the implications examined carefully. In this particular situation, the discovery may well be achieved more wisely by not telling the truth about what has happened that evening, even if directly challenged. It may be better that he exercise the virtue of discretion at this stage and say "only what is helpful for building others up according to their needs, that it may benefit those who listen."

Desmond feels that it would be wise to show some patience and self-control and aim to talk to Terry alone at the first opportunity, to try to discover if the allegations are true and how much Alice knows about them. He will then have more of an idea of the best way to proceed with this tangle, without risking the destruction of their marriage and their fledgling faith, and his credibility as a pastor in the town. If the allegation is untrue, then this potentially damaging situation also needs to be dealt with as swiftly as wisdom allows.

wrestling with life's tough issues

Desmond looks at his motives

The Ephesians passage is clearly a challenge not just to conform to rules about outward behavior and to avoid telling lies, but also to consider motives and the development of character. Desmond is to "put off" his old self and "be made new" in the attitude of his mind. The aim of his ethical life is to be "created to be like God in true righteousness and holiness" (4:22, 24).

When Desmond looks at himself with honesty, he sees that there is quite a lot of anger inside, opening the possibility of some sort of malice in his desire to confront Terry. He also discovers an element of self-satisfaction, because from the first time he met Terry he rather disliked him. This desire to expose the truth about Terry's life should be tempered by humility (he might be wrong in this judgment), by kindness, and by a readiness to believe the best and to forgive. It would be good to overcome his anger before doing

Desmond knows that having the virtue of honesty involves a deep concern for the truth, so it is most important that the true situation is discovered and the implications examined carefully.

anything, so that he can "speak the truth in love" and be an "imitator of God" in the way he responds to the situation.

Desmond is aware that he has a special role in the community, which affects how he applies the virtue of honesty in this situation. He has a pastoral responsibility to both Alice and Terry, to do all he can to protect their marriage, to bring them into the church, and to build them up toward Christian maturity. He also has a responsibility to the rest of the Christian community, to teach and model the Christian virtues and to try to keep "unity in the faith."

Repeating the yet unproven allegations against Terry in front of Alice that evening seems to him to be failing in his pastoral responsibilities to both of them and to the community that he leads. On the other hand, it seems equally irresponsible for him to allow them to take part in a baptism service without making any response to the allegations he has heard.

Desmond's conclusion

Desmond decides that he will pray hard for the gift of love and self-control and, at the meeting that evening, ask Terry and Alice to give him a few more days to check the practical arrangements for a baptism next month before they confirm the date with their relatives and friends. If pressed about these arrangements, he can say something about the organist's, or his own, availability.

He will otherwise conduct the evening as if nothing has happened and, however directly he is questioned, he will not be pressured into revealing the allegations that have been made to him. Even if this does not mean telling any direct lies, he deeply regrets the deception it will involve, but he believes that in this situation it is the wisest way in which to pursue and commend the virtue of honesty, and to exercise his pastoral care of this couple and of the community.

The day after the meeting, he will speak to Terry alone as soon as he can and, once he knows more about the situation, let those insights guide how he proceeds.

wrestling with life's tough issues

Wisdom

In Desmond's dilemma about telling the truth, looking for consequences did not seem to be very helpful. Not only did the important virtue of honesty seem to drop out of the picture, but he also appeared to end up with no clear guidance about what to do. His course of action may have been similar to that reached by considering virtues, but his reasons for taking that course of action and his confidence in it would not have been as strong.

Christians will probably be divided about whether the virtue of honesty is, in this situation, best expressed and promoted by simply keeping the rule and telling the truth regardless of the consequences, or by Desmond's use of his practical moral wisdom in deciding not to reveal what has happened until he has more information. Whether this idea of practical moral wisdom, which is so important for Virtue Ethics, is also recommended in the Bible is a question we shall now explore.

There is a thread running through the Bible which suggests that righteousness—living well—involves more than the exercise of intellect and will, more than knowing what the rules are and keeping them. It is, rather, a practical skill that comes with maturity, a skill that is gained through training, imitation, and experience. The word used for this skill, in the Bible and in Virtue Ethics, is "wisdom." We could describe it as the ability to make good plans and be successful in achieving good outcomes.

WISDOM IN THE OLD TESTAMENT

In Exodus 28, the Lord gives instructions to "all the skilled men to whom I have given wisdom in such matters that they are to make garments for Aaron" (v. 3). These men are given a practical skill for garment making. Solomon is given skills for ruling God's people, for diplomacy, for understanding life and human nature (1 Kings 3 and 10), some of which he records in the books of

Proverbs and Ecclesiastes (although, as far as some aspects of his private life were concerned, Solomon showed a singular lack of wisdom: see 1 Kings 11).

In the Bible, wisdom is primarily a characteristic of God and then, as we saw above, a gift that he gives to people. Job is one of those who witness to God's wisdom, and his knowledge of it sustains him through his misfortunes. In Job 28:23–28 we read, "God understands the way to [wisdom] and he alone knows where it dwells. . . . When he established the force of the wind and measured out the waters . . . he looked at wisdom and appraised it; he confirmed it and tested it. And he said to man, 'The fear of the Lord—that is wisdom, and to shun evil is understanding.'"

In the "Wisdom literature" of the Bible,[34] this attribute of God is sometimes poetically personified as a female figure. In Proverbs 8, Wisdom calls out: "Choose my instruction instead of silver . . . for wisdom is more precious than rubies, and nothing you can desire can compare with her. . . . I love those who love me, and those who seek me find me" (vv. 10–11, 17). The woman Wisdom goes on to say that the Lord brought her forth "as the first of his works"; she was "appointed from eternity" (vv. 22–23). "I was there when he set the heavens in place, when he marked out the horizon on the face of the deep. . . . I was the craftsman at his side.

The word used for this skill, in the Bible and in Virtue Ethics, is "wisdom." We could describe it as the ability to make good plans and be successful in achieving good outcomes.

I was filled with delight day after day, rejoicing always in his presence . . . whoever finds me finds life" (vv. 27, 30, 35).

Wisdom, in the sense of the practical skill of right living, begins with "the fear of the Lord" and "knowledge of the Holy One" (Proverbs 9:10). It comes as a gift from God, through the experience of living with him. In contrast, worldly wisdom is doomed to fail. "The wisdom of the wise will perish, the intelligence of the intelligent will vanish. Woe to those who go to great depths to hide their plans from the Lord, who do their work in darkness and think, 'Who sees us? Who will know?'" (Isaiah 29:14–15).

WISDOM IN THE NEW TESTAMENT

This background from the Old Testament helps us to understand the use of the idea of wisdom in the ethical teaching of the New Testament, because

wrestling with life's tough issues

all the same ideas are taken up there. Paul refers to God as the "only wise God" (Romans 16:27) and praises "the depth of the riches of the wisdom and knowledge of God" (Romans 11:33). The people who meet Jesus are amazed by his wisdom (Matthew 13:54).

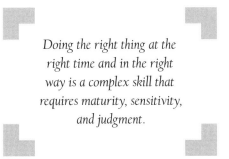

Doing the right thing at the right time and in the right way is a complex skill that requires maturity, sensitivity, and judgment.

James tells us that the practical skill of wisdom is a gift that God gives to those who ask him: "If any of you lacks wisdom, he should ask God, who gives generously to all without finding fault, and it will be given to him" (James 1:5).

Christ takes over the roles of the Old Testament figure of Wisdom. He is described as "the firstborn over all creation" and the agency through whom God creates and sustains the world (Colossians 1:15–16). Paul gives him the title of "the wisdom of God" (1 Corinthians 1:24).

As in the Old Testament, worldly wisdom is contrasted with godly wisdom. Paul quotes Isaiah 29:14 and says that God has "made foolish the wisdom of the world" (1 Corinthians 1:20).

WISDOM IN VIRTUE ETHICS

Wisdom is an important idea in Virtue Ethics, too. This approach to ethics emphasizes that right living involves a great deal more than knowing some rules and having a strong enough will to keep them. It acknowledges that real situations are complicated and that making ethical decisions and implementing them successfully is a difficult business. Doing the right thing at the right time and in the right way is a complex skill that requires maturity, sensitivity, and judgment. It requires not only that we have the right values, feelings, and intentions to choose the right action, but also that we have the wisdom to do it in the right way for the particular situation.

Having honesty as a virtue means more than telling the truth, sometimes with "gritted teeth," against one's natural judgment or feelings, simply because lying is perceived to be forbidden. People with the virtue of honesty live transparent lives because they have developed honesty as part of their character; they love the truth and feel regret at any kind of deception. Their sense of values gives them wise judgment about how much honesty is appropriate in a particular situation, so that they avoid the vices of either too little honesty (deception, unreliability, duplicity, and so on) or too much (unkindness, indiscretion, rudeness, and so on). It is the same for other virtues: generosity, for example, can turn out to be patronizing, profligate, or manipulating if expressed unwisely.

Wisdom is what enables virtuous people to "get it right" in particular circumstances. Being honest involves reading the situation correctly and having some emotional empathy. It also involves making the right judgments about how much honesty is appropriate, or whether it needs to be balanced with loyalty, faithfulness to a confidence or a promise, kindness, protection from harm, or making the most of an opportunity to do good.

This sort of wisdom comes from experience of life and an understanding of human nature. It grows slowly in the right environment, with the right models, training, intention, and experience. Virtuous people not only tell the truth, they tell it wisely—appropriately, kindly, and effectively.

DOES PAUL RECOMMEND THIS SORT OF WISDOM?

Can we see this idea of wisdom—a practical skill in ethical living—being recommended in the New Testament? In particular, is it fair to interpret Paul's exhortation to "Be very careful, then, how you live—not as unwise but as wise, making the most of every opportunity, because the days are evil" (Ephesians 5:15–16), as reflecting this sort of approach?

I would like to suggest that we can—that all these ideas about living well are present in the New Testament's, and particularly in Paul's, approach to ethics. Paul uses the word "wisdom" liberally in both his theology and his call to moral living. For example, he says in Romans 16:19, "I want you to be wise about what is good, and innocent about what is evil," and in Colossians 4:5, "Be wise in the way you act toward outsiders; make the most of every opportunity."

Paul firmly connects right living with identifying what is worthwhile and important. To him, this is supremely the gospel of Jesus. Paul was prepared to "become all things to all men so that by all possible means I might save some. I do all this," he says, "for the sake of the gospel" (1 Corinthians 9:22–23).

Paul also sees that particular ethical decisions have to be made in complex situations. Much of his ethical teaching is given in the form of examples of his own wisdom in applying the Christian virtues to particular situations. In 1 Corinthians 10:23–30, Paul gives advice about how the Christians in Corinth are to behave with regard to buying and eating meat from pagan markets. "'Everything is permissible,'" he tells them, "but not everything is

wrestling with life's tough issues

beneficial. 'Everything is permissible'—but not everything is constructive. Nobody should seek his own good, but the good of others" (1 Corinthians 10:23–24).

Paul then unravels his own wisdom for this situation. Doing what is right here can be resolved not with rules but with sensitivity and maturity and a firm sense of what is ultimately worthwhile: "Do it all for the glory of God. Do not cause anyone to stumble, whether Jews, Greeks or the church of God" (vv. 31–32).

JESUS TALKS ABOUT WISDOM

We have already seen Jesus' emphasis on character rather than action in the Sermon on the Mount. The sermon concludes with Jesus saying that the wise man is the one who "hears these words of mine and puts them into practice" (Matthew 7:24).

Jesus also makes an interesting remark about wisdom in Matthew 11:19. He is responding to the fact that John the Baptist had been criticized for his ascetic lifestyle while he, Jesus, was being criticized for "eating and drinking" and being "a

> *The sermon concludes with Jesus saying that the wise man is the one who "hears these words of mine and puts them into practice" (Matthew 7:24).*

friend of sinners." Knowing the right way to behave in these different situations is not a matter of rules, Jesus seems to be saying, "But wisdom is proved right by her actions."

JAMES ON WISDOM

The letter of James perhaps explains this approach most clearly. In the context of telling the Christian community how to respond to persecution, he urges them to ask for wisdom from God, "who gives generously to all without finding fault" (1:5). James puts wisdom firmly in the area of right living when he says:

> Who is wise and understanding among you? Let him show it by his good life, by deeds done in the humility that comes from wisdom. But if you harbor bitter envy and selfish ambition in your hearts, do not boast about it or deny

the truth. Such "wisdom" does not come down from heaven but is earthly, unspiritual, of the devil. For where you have envy and selfish ambition, there you find disorder and every evil practice. But the wisdom that comes from heaven is first of all pure; then peace-loving, considerate, submissive, full of mercy and good fruit, impartial and sincere. (James 3:13–17)

Once again, coming to the Bible with the insights of Virtue Ethics helps to illuminate and clarify for us this characteristic of wisdom, which is so important to moral living.

10

Charlotte faces an unplanned pregnancy and looks at Romans 13

CHARLOTTE'S STORY

Charlotte and Justin have been married for nine years, and they have two girls, who are five and three. Although Justin would have liked a son, they have decided not to have any more children because Charlotte's health was not good during her pregnancies and they feel that a larger family would be a bit of a strain on their family finances.

Justin's mother, Grace, is approaching her 70th birthday when she is diagnosed with an inoperable cancer. After much family discussion, Charlotte has agreed that she and Justin will take Grace to Canada for a final visit to her other son and his family so that they can all celebrate her birthday together. On their return, Grace will move into their home, where Charlotte, who is a trained nurse, will care for and nurse her.

The hotel and flights are already booked when Charlotte suspects and then quickly confirms that her contraceptives have let her down and she is pregnant. By the time of the planned visit to Canada, she will be too far advanced in her pregnancy to take a long airplane flight safely, and, with a new baby, she feels that she will have neither the room nor the time and energy to take over the care of her mother-in-law. She keeps this to herself because she can't imagine how she could go about telling Justin or his mother.

CHARLOTTE TURNS TO THE BIBLE

Charlotte is overwhelmed by conflicting thoughts and feelings that pull her this way and that. In her daily Bible readings she comes to a passage in Romans 13 about love. Perhaps this can help her to make the right decision. She reads:

Let no debt remain outstanding, except the continuing debt to love one another, for he who loves his fellowman has fulfilled the law. The commandments, "Do not commit adultery," "Do not murder," "Do not steal," "Do not covet," and whatever other commandment there may be, are summed up in this one rule: "Love your neighbor as yourself." Love does no harm to its neighbor. Therefore love is the fulfillment of the law.

And do this, understanding the present time. The hour has come for you to wake up from your slumber, because our salvation is nearer now than when we first believed. The night is nearly over; the day is almost here. So let us put aside the deeds of darkness and put on the armor of light. Let us behave decently, as in the daytime, not in orgies and drunkenness, not in sexual immorality and debauchery, not in dissension and jealousy. Rather, clothe yourselves with the Lord Jesus Christ, and do not think about how to gratify the desires of the sinful nature. (Romans 13:8–14)

THREE APPROACHES TO SOLVING THE PROBLEM

LOOKING AT CONSEQUENCES

Charlotte wonders if this passage is describing the ethics that looks at consequences, which she learned about in her high school Religious Studies classes. Is Paul saying here that New Testament ethics overturns the Old Testament ethics of rules—that as a Christian she should resolve her present dilemma by trying to be as impartial as she can and deciding what course of action would lead to the best outcomes for everyone who will be affected by what she does?

Charlotte is overwhelmed by conflicting thoughts and feelings that pull her this way and that. In her daily Bible readings she comes to a passage in Romans 13 about love.

"I have to act as though I love them all as much as I love myself, and do no harm to any of them," she thinks. "That is more important than any rules about killing." Once she has done some calculations about the different consequences, all she will need is the willpower to do what is right rather than following her own feelings or desires.

She begins to think everything through, but it is not as easy as she thought it might be. If she decides to go ahead and have the baby, Justin's mother and the rest of her family will be devastated. All their carefully made plans for

Grace's birthday visit to Canada and future care at Charlotte's home will be ruined. She will have to go back on what she said she would do and withdraw her offer to look after Grace in her home. Charlotte has never been her mother-in-law's favorite, and Justin tends to take his mother's side. This course of action can only cause harm by upsetting Grace and aggravating the tensions within the family.

Asking if they can move the trip forward will irritate and inconvenience everyone, and will mean wasting money—something that both Justin and his brother will object to. Justin is not used to having the girls on his own, and Charlotte knows that he would not consider taking them and his mother without her. The girls will lose the chance of a great vacation and are looking forward to having Granny to live with them. The family will have to start thinking again about nursing homes, which both Grace and her sons were very much against, as it will mean that her small inheritance will get used up on nursing home costs.

If Charlotte concentrates on consequences, how could it be right to cause this much harm and distress to so many people? If she truly loves them, she would not choose this course of action. If she has the baby, the only person who will experience good consequences is herself, because, although she had not planned to get pregnant, she now feels very strongly that she doesn't want to destroy the new life developing within her. Although the family had agreed it was the best plan for them all, nursing her mother-in-law was not what she would ideally have planned for the next years of her life.

If she has the baby, the only person who will experience good consequences is herself, because, although she had not planned to get pregnant, she now feels very strongly that she doesn't want to destroy the new life developing within her.

If no one knows . . .

Another alternative is to terminate the pregnancy as soon as she can: it is still quite early. In fact, it is still within the first trimester. This option goes against her natural feelings and may cause upset to some of the family, especially Justin, who will have to cope with a personal loss to himself, especially if this baby turns out to be a boy. Grace will be put in a difficult position, knowing that it is for her sake that this choice of action has been taken. But what if Charlotte could organize the termination secretly? If no one ever finds out what she has done, no harm will come to anyone but herself. Charlotte knows of a clinic that asks few questions, and she has money of her own available. She believes that this course of action may be possible and that she could do it quite quickly.

Charlotte thinks through the possibility that this early fetus may count, in the moral sense, as a person—someone with the same rights as the other people she has considered in her calculations. In the talks and discussions she has been in at church, however, people have expressed different ideas about this. Some people thought that the fetus is a "person" from the moment of conception, but others didn't, and the Bible didn't seem to be very clear about it. She is reluctant to accept that her faulty birth control could destroy so many lives. Although this fact concerning the status of the fetus seems crucial to her calculations, she can't see how to resolve it or how to get her head around the idea of the fetus, at this stage, "wanting" or "not wanting" to be born.

> *Charlotte thinks through the possibility that this early fetus may count, in the moral sense, as a person.*

Charlotte's conclusion

Armed with the ideas of the ethics of consequences, Charlotte sees Romans 13 to be saying that the old commandments, with their prohibition on killing, are overturned by the idea of loving others, of caring for their well-being. This, for her, means acting in a way that maximizes their personal happiness. She concludes that, in this situation, love for her husband's family means that it is right for her to destroy this fetus, which she decides not to bring into the calculations because it is not yet capable of having conscious feelings about itself or its own happiness.

Charlotte knows that it will be very hard on her to go through with this decision on her own, but, because it represents the best outcome for everyone else, love requires that she must not put her own desires above her family's good. Perhaps she will be able to persuade Justin to have another baby after his mother's death.

LOOKING FOR RULES

Many people will be thinking that this is not what Paul meant and that Charlotte's decision is not a good one. By concentrating merely on the consequences of her actions, the virtue of honesty, the importance of her own value and feelings, and the seriousness of taking the life of a human fetus seem to have dropped out of Charlotte's calculations. So what has gone wrong, and what happens if Charlotte does not have the idea in her mind that we need to think only about consequences in moral decision-making, but instead goes to the Bible looking for a universal rule that will solve her dilemma?

She will notice at once that Paul says that the commandment "Do not murder" is one of those that can be summed up in the one rule, "Love your neighbor as yourself," and she can see that if we care about another person in the way that we care about ourselves, thoughts of killing them will never arise. She remembers Jesus' warning that the commandment not to murder also prohibits angry feelings or harsh words to other people (Matthew 5:21–22). She has no ill will toward the fetus growing within her, and she is sure that if it continues to develop she will come to love it—but does the rule about not committing murder apply in this situation?

Charlotte can see several significant differences between an early fetus and an independently living child. Must she—can she—feel about the life of this tiny, unseen, unformed thing that has the potential to become a person, in the way she feels about her own life or the life of her two daughters? If she could, if this was appropriate, she would not want it killed, but she is not sure that a very early fetus does count as a neighbor in this way.

Some different opinions

Charlotte knows that the Roman Catholic Church says that the prohibition of murder covers the medical termination of pregnancy at any stage, on the basis that the fetus is, in the moral sense, a person from the moment of conception. She also knows that this is the opinion of her pastor and most of the people in her church. On the other hand, she knows that some Christians, even some biblical scholars, disagree with this view.

She can't think of any Bible passages that say one way or the other in a straightforward manner—and she is not surprised, since at the time the Bible was written people did not know what happened in the very early months of pregnancy. But then, nothing she can find from today's knowledge about the development of early fetuses helps her to decide when it becomes a person, either. Charlotte ends up not sure that the universal rule in the Bible about illegitimately taking the life of another human being does apply to a very early fetus.

She sees that Paul says she is not to "gratify the desires of the sinful nature," but her natural desire is to keep the baby, and this does not seem to her to be sinful at all.

Charlotte's conclusion

Charlotte decides that her search for a clear universal rule in the Bible about the termination of pregnancy has come to a dead end, but, impressed by the seriousness of the command not to take life, she decides that she must keep the baby, whatever the consequences are for the rest of her family.

LOOKING FOR VIRTUES

In both of the previous approaches to Charlotte's situation, one of the most important factors has turned out to be the status of the fetus she is carrying: is it a neighbor competing with others in its right to happiness, or a human being, protected by the rules against murder? In the first event, the seriousness of taking the life of a fetus seemed to get ignored, and in the second, the consequences for her family were similarly forgotten— as well as the import of Romans 13, which seems at the very least to be saying that the principles of the law should always be applied in ways that reflect love.

> *She can't imagine Jesus as a pregnant 21st-century woman, but she can think about the virtues that his life displayed and how they might relate to this situation.*

Some people may feel that one or the other of these decisions is right, but in neither case has the Bible passage helped her very much in reaching it.

So what happens if Charlotte comes to the same passage in Romans, looking for help to see what a virtuous person would do in this situation? Can she find ways of using this situation to develop into a more virtuous person and promote virtuous living in her world? She may notice the words in the final sentence: "Clothe yourself with the Lord Jesus Christ." She can't imagine Jesus as a pregnant 21st-century woman, but she can think about the virtues that his life displayed and how they might relate to this situation.

Developing a loving nature

Seeing the passage as an expression of Virtue Ethics, Charlotte can see that love, in the sense of benevolence or care for others, is what you might call a foundational virtue that stands behind the commandments mentioned by Paul. The love that God models to us leads directly toward faithfulness, gentleness, honesty, and contentment. So she wonders if Paul is saying that living as a Christian is not just about keeping rules in an external way but about developing a loving nature, which freely expresses itself in these other virtues so that the commandments are willingly and joyfully kept?

A virtuous person is, then, not someone who merely acts right, sometimes through gritted teeth, but someone who feels and thinks right. This kind of person is one who can examine and evaluate their feelings, whose thinking can be guided by the calculation of consequences, by useful rules, and, most importantly, by a sense of values—ideas about what is worthwhile in life and what is trivial or unimportant.

Christian love must be deeper and broader than merely wanting people to get what they want, or even than caring about their well-being.

Charlotte notices that as Paul goes on with his advice in this passage, he mentions some vices—drunkenness, immorality, dissension, and jealousy. These are character traits that come from an unloving nature and are inappropriate for a Christian. Christian love must be deeper and broader than merely wanting people to get what they want, or even than caring about their well-being. We can't have a loving nature, in the Christian sense, without also being self-controlled, faithful, peaceable, and content. So how would someone with these virtues act in this situation?

The passage helps Charlotte to think more carefully about the virtue of love, which Paul recommends so strongly here. Having the virtue of love involves having the practical wisdom to know that even feelings of love can go wrong. Love can be too strong or too weak for a particular situation. It can be felt or expressed inappropriately. A love of others that leads us to ignore totally our own welfare for relatively trivial ends, or to ignore important virtues like honesty or faithfulness, has turned into enslavement or even idolatry. A love that makes it impossible to tell the truth or do what we deeply feel to be right has become a sort of cowardice. Although Charlotte clearly has some responsibility for the care of her mother-in-law, she finds that she needs to think about whether she is allowing herself to be taken advantage of by Grace's children, who really have the greater responsibility.

Some other virtues to consider

Charlotte will certainly want to consider the virtue of honesty. A virtuous person would not want to get into a serious situation of deception with their nearest and dearest. Paul talks here and elsewhere about living in the light—living open, transparent lives. She was trying to think impartially, but in fact she has a special relationship with her husband and a special responsibility toward her marriage. She needs to think very carefully about how terminating the pregnancy without telling anyone would involve both deception and even a kind of unfaithfulness. It might damage her marriage and some of her other close relationships, and these are things that she values highly.

When Charlotte considers the commandments that Paul mentions and asks herself how these rules can help her to behave virtuously, she can see that the commandment about murder points to the unique significance of a human life and thus to the seriousness of ending a life—even a potential, or not yet fully formed, human life. Although it is, in several ways, not the same as a more developed fetus or an independently living child, and although she may not feel any bond with it yet, over the next few months feelings of affection and care could grow, and in time it could become another member of her family. Looking from this perspective, Charlotte finds that she does not have to decide at what exact moment a fetus becomes a person as though it were a fact that makes all the difference. She can appreciate that the nature of a fetus is something that changes during a pregnancy, and the feelings and actions that are appropriate toward it change too.

These thoughts about the old commandment help Charlotte to distinguish what is worthwhile and serious from what is relatively unimportant. She decides that it is much more important to allow the baby to be born than to take on responsibility for the care of her mother-in-law, which other people can do. Other people may have serious reasons to terminate a pregnancy, but it is not the sort of thing that should be done lightly.

The good that Charlotte would be maximizing by having a secret abortion is the personal happiness of others—seeing that the people she is bound up with in her family get what she thinks they want. But the story of Jesus leads her to question this idea of what "good" means. For a Christian, there must be a deeper sense of a good life than this. (Might it actually be a good thing for her mother-in-law not to get her own way all the time?) She decides that the best way to promote the ultimate good of herself, her marriage, her unborn child, and everyone else is to follow her own practical wisdom in this situation, informed as it is by her knowledge of the nature of God's love.

Charlotte's conclusion

Approaching the passage like this helps Charlotte to recognize her reluctance to break the news to Justin and his mother as cowardice, and her strong

wrestling with life's tough issues

feelings about keeping the baby as appropriate regard for herself and the new life within her. The love she is pursuing as a Christian is God's love, which is filled out by other virtues—honesty, courage, faithfulness to her marriage vows, an appropriate feeling for the significance of a developing human life, a sense of her own worth, and concern about the ultimate good—rather than the immediate personal happiness of those around her.

Acting out of this sort of love, and with regret for the harm that will be done and the need to go back on her word, as well as with some moral courage, she decides to talk to Justin. She will say that she thinks the right thing to do is to tell his mother and the rest of the family that they will have to make other plans for the trip to Canada and for Grace's care, because her contraceptives have let her down and they are having an unplanned baby.

> *The love she is pursuing as a Christian is God's love, which is filled out by other virtues.*

Love

IN THE PREVIOUS CHAPTER CHARLOTTE tried to consider what would be the most loving thing to do. Jesus is probably best known for his explanation of his own mission: "God so loved the world that he gave his one and only Son" (John 3:16); his parting words to his disciples, "My command is this: Love each other as I have loved you" (John 15:12); and his summary of the law: "'Love the Lord your God with all your heart and with all your soul and with all your strength and with all your mind'; and, 'Love your neighbor as yourself'" (Luke 10:27), which is followed by the story of the good Samaritan. You could conclude that Jesus taught that love is the basis of all God's dealings with humankind and is all that God requires of Christians in their ethical living.

The epistles echo this emphasis, Paul telling us, "The entire law is summed up in a single command: 'Love your neighbor as yourself'" (Galatians 5:14), and John declaring, "Love comes from God. Everyone who loves has been born of God and knows God. Whoever does not love does not know God, because God is love" (1 John 4:7–8).

The first question we must now consider is: does a "rules" approach to ethics adequately reflect this emphasis? We then need to ask: since this emphasis on love seems to encompass an attitude of benevolence toward one's neighbor, can it be interpreted as a "consequences" approach to ethics, of the sort proposed by J. S. Mill and applied to Christian ethics by Joseph Fletcher and John Robinson?[35] Alternatively, do the approaches of Virtue Ethics capture it in a more constructive and helpful way?

THE COMMAND TO LOVE

In John's Gospel, Jesus says to his disciples, "If you love me, you will obey what I command" (14:15), and later, "If you obey my commands, you will remain in my love, just as I have obeyed my Father's commands and remain in his love. I have told you this so that my joy may be in you and that your joy may be complete" (15:10–11). These words may seem to indicate that loving God and neighbor involves a "rules" approach to living well—keeping the commandments. We need to notice, however, that Jesus goes straight on to say, "My command is this: Love each other as I have loved you" (15:12). In John's Gospel, this is Jesus' only commandment other than the command to believe in him (6:29).

> *Both Jesus and Paul teach that love, in some sense, encompasses and fulfills the law.*

It is certainly easy for a "rules" approach to become an unloving one. In Matthew's Gospel, Jesus tells the teachers of the law and the Pharisees, who "sit in Moses' seat," that they use the law to "tie up heavy loads and put them on men's shoulders" and to "shut the kingdom of heaven in men's faces," while they neglect "the more important matters of the law—justice, mercy and faithfulness" (Matthew 23:2, 4, 13, 23).

Both Jesus and Paul teach that love, in some sense, encompasses and fulfills the law (Luke 10:26–28; Romans 13:8–10). In an ongoing dispute in our church last week, we were urged to try to resolve the conflict at the level of principles rather than people, because, we were told, making it personal fudges and obscures the clarity needed for debates of this kind. But can this be right for a Christian community which believes that to love our fellow human beings is to fulfill the law, that all the commandments are summed up in the one rule: "Love your neighbor as yourself"?

WILL RULES DO?

Although some Christians are happy using rules to make their ethical decisions, invoking an absolute, universal rule in complex situations does seem to many to be a tricky business, because it does not always reflect the complexity of the situation and can so easily lead to actions that are graceless and unloving.

We can see the difficulties that arise with complex situations when we try to apply the absolute rule of not killing in the context of early abortion. Very early fetuses are different in several significant ways from more developed ones, and more developed fetuses are different from independently living, self-conscious human beings already existing in a network of relationships. In our society, this is recognized in the wide acceptance of the coil and the

wrestling with life's tough issues

"morning after" pill as methods of contraception, the natural preference for saving a mother rather than an early fetus in a medical emergency, and the growing trend for holding funerals after late miscarriages or stillbirths.

It is very hard to get from the facts we know about the development of fetuses to a firm decision about the exact point at which the rule of not killing human beings starts to apply. At the same time, if we insist that the rule about not killing any fetus be imposed on an unwilling young victim of rape, or a woman suffering from ill health and poverty who already has more children than she can adequately care for, we do seem to be open to the accusation of putting heavy loads on other people's shoulders and neglecting the more important matters of justice, mercy, and faithfulness (Matthew 23:4, 23).

So, if there are difficulties in accepting the full impact of the New Testament's emphasis on love while applying an ethic of rules, does this mean that Christians are to embrace a "consequences" approach to ethics—to decide on the right course of action by calculating the consequences for everyone affected by them, asking themselves what they think others would want them to do or what they would want others to do for them, and then taking the course of action that maximizes happiness?

Jesus says in Matthew 7:12, "Do to others what you would have them do to you, for this sums up the Law and the Prophets," and Paul repeats this teaching: "Love does no harm to its neighbor. Therefore love is the fulfillment of the law" (Romans 13:10).

Is BENEVOLENCE ALL WE NEED?

These two statements seem to confirm that caring for the well-being of others—what we might see as the virtue of benevolence—is all that is needed for Christian righteousness. We saw in the last chapter, however, that when Charlotte tried to use this idea to decide about a termination of her pregnancy, the result proved unsatisfactory because several important aspects of the situation were neglected. It seemed possible for her to miss the significance of the rule not to kill (some might prefer to say, the principle behind the rule—that human life is immensely valuable and should not be taken for trivial reasons). It also seemed possible for her to ignore the important rule about not being dishonest (some might prefer to say, the virtue of honesty). If loving God with all our heart and soul and loving our neighbor as ourselves can summarize the whole law, it must mean more than just acting benevolently.

Is it, then, possible to argue that a Virtue Ethics approach leads us to understand better what this emphasis on love as the central Christian virtue means in practice—what it would most probably have meant when it was written and first read? I believe that this is the case, firstly because the ethics of rules and the ethics of consequences both concentrate on achieving right actions, while the Christian ethics of love and the ethics of virtue both concentrate on achieving right character. The aim of Christian holiness is not always to act in a loving way but rather to develop a loving nature. It can be argued that feelings cannot be commanded, but Paul's ethics are not about feelings. Nor are they about either following rules or making impartial calculations.

In the New Testament, we start our growth in Christian holiness by receiving God's love and, by his grace, learning to return it (1 John 4:19–21). It is this that gives us the grace and courage to develop our character so that we do not just act benevolently but really love our fellow Christians and even our enemies. New Testament ethics is essentially about working with the Spirit of God as he produces his fruit in us. On our part, we must continually weed out and destroy our vices—crucifying "the sinful nature with its passions and desires"—and must recognize and nurture the Christian virtues so that we become increasingly mature, holy, loving people (Galatians 5:22–25).

> *A Virtue Ethics approach leads us to understand better what this emphasis on love as the central Christian virtue means in practice—what it would most probably have meant when it was written and first read?*

Secondly, when we are concentrating on virtues rather than rules, the Christian call to love all our fellow human beings can be seen to extend in appropriate ways to the rest of God's creation. We can see that it is not the case that killing all human beings is wrong and killing everything else is fine, which is where a "rules" approach can lead us. If we have developed a loving nature, the difficulties involved in establishing the status (person or not person) of a newly conceived embryo, or of someone being kept alive on a life-support system, or even an animal or a tree, will not stop us from recognizing their value. It may be a different value from the value of a fully conscious human being, but it can nevertheless invoke in us an appropriate sense of respect and care.

QUESTIONS ABOUT STATUS AND RIGHTS

Seen from either "rules" or "consequence" approaches, questions about the status of fetuses at different times during pregnancy, and questions about the conflicting rights of the mother and the fetus, take center stage, but the answers to these questions seem always to elude us. Medical aids, like the improved technology that clearly reveals the appearance of early fetuses, and biblical texts like Psalm 51:5 ("Surely I have been a sinner from birth, sinful from the time my mother conceived me") help us to see that fetuses have a special value and require special treatment. They do not, however, enable us to decide whether, at a particular point in their development, they count as human beings for the purpose of applying the rule "Do not kill."

From a Virtue Ethics perspective, these difficult questions about the status of fetuses at different stages of development fade in importance. So do questions about whether women have the right to do what they want with their own bodies. Women may have that right, but some things may be more important than merely exercising our rights.

Instead, the moral questions surrounding abortion become whether, taking into consideration things like the value of a human fetus and the consequences of one's action, terminating this pregnancy in this particular (and probably complex) situation is an action that is loving, wise, brave, patient, honest, generous, and so on, and whether it expresses and promotes the community's ideas about what is important in life—what a good life and a good society are. From this perspective, we can see that some things, even if they are experienced as harm, are relatively trivial and some things are worthwhile even if they bring some pain and hardship with them.

Special responsibilities

In the application of universal rules and in the calculation of consequences, everyone is meant to count equally, including ourselves. Virtue Ethics helps in our understanding of Christian love, however, because its practical wisdom points us to the value of special relationships, which bring special responsibilities. The call to care for our children, our parents, our students, employees, or congregations carries greater weight than the call to care for strangers, although that call comes too, especially if the stranger is sleeping on our doorstep (see Jesus' parable in Luke 16:19–31).

In Ephesians 6, Paul emphasizes the special responsibilities inherent in families and employment. Virtue Ethics approaches capture this emphasis better than rules or consequences approaches, because in complex situations we need wisdom in the way we think about love rather than just the ability to recognize rules or to calculate impartially and maximize general happiness.

THE RICH CONTENT OF CHRISTIAN LOVE

Virtue Ethics emphasizes the connection between all the virtues, and this helps us to grasp that the virtue of love in the New Testament is always filled out with a rich content. Christian love is not practiced in a vacuum, as if nothing but benevolence mattered, as if a happy outcome for everyone means everything, and honesty, justice, faithfulness, and so on are expendable.

The meaning of love is explained and exemplified for Christians in God's dealing with his people and ultimately in Jesus' life and death. Paul uses this story to inspire the Christian virtues in us (see, for example, Philippians 2:5–11) and fills out the meaning of love for us in passages like 1 Corinthians 13, where he says, "Love is patient, love is kind. It does not envy, it does not boast, it is not proud. It is not rude, it is not self-seeking, it is not easily angered, it keeps no record of wrongs. Love does not delight in evil but rejoices with the truth. It always protects, always trusts, always hopes, always perseveres" (vv. 4–7).

In Romans, Paul says, "Love must be sincere. Hate what is evil; cling to what is good." He then continues by recommending a host of virtues that reflect the teaching in the Sermon on the Mount: joy, patience, faithfulness, gentleness, humility, mercy, and peace (12:9–21).

> The meaning of love is explained and exemplified for Christians in God's dealing with his people and ultimately in Jesus' life and death.

To love one's neighbor can be seen as simply to wish them happiness or, in an entirely negative way, not to cause them any harm. This seems to be the basis of much unreflective secular morality today. When, however, we model our love on God's love for his creation and his faithfulness to his people, when our thinking is molded by the story of Jesus' life and death for us on the cross, we have to think a great deal deeper about what love means.

Jesus said, "Blessed are those who mourn" and "Blessed are those who are persecuted" (Matthew 5:4, 10), while Paul says that suffering produces perseverance, and perseverance produces character (Romans 5:3–4). This is a rather different set of values to guide Christians in their moral wisdom. Personal happiness—people getting what they think they want—cannot in this context be seen as the ultimate good that love desires for oneself or for others.

Perhaps Christians could change the goalposts and aim to act so as to maximize the ultimate good—the flourishing, in an informed Christian sense, of everyone affected by their actions. The most straightforward way, surely the only practical way, of doing this is by pursuing the virtues, pursuing God's own nature in our own lives and communities. This is not the ethics of rules or of consequences. This is the ethics of virtue.

12

Alice considers going on a peace march and looks at Philippians 4

ALICE'S STORY

Alice is in her last year of high school and plans to go on to college to study medicine. Her father is approaching retirement from a lifetime in the army. After many moves, they have settled in London, where Alice has joined the senior class at a private school. A new friend invited her to a Bible study group at the school and, through that, to a local church, where she has become a Christian and been baptized, somewhat to the puzzlement and apprehension of her parents. She and her father seem to manage to disagree, often loudly, on almost everything. Her mother finds this very trying.

Alice is particularly enthusiastic about the school Bible study group. They try to apply the Bible to world events and, in the aftermath of the destruction of the World Trade Center in New York and the subsequent invasion of Iraq they have been looking at the subject of war and peace. Alice was very disturbed by the TV pictures of the Twin Towers coming down and, living in London, is anxious about the possibility of terrorist reprisals. She reads all she can about the "war on terror" and has stopped using the subway for her daily journey to school.

The Bible study group tackles Romans 13. Some of the girls have read about the theory of "just war" proposed by the early Church Fathers Ambrose (339–397) and Augustine (354–430). They come to the opinion that America and Britain can't claim in this situation to be "agent[s] of God's wrath to bring punishment on the wrongdoer" (Romans 13:4) and that the war with Iraq is not, according to this theory, legitimate. They are not all convinced, but the more articulate girls feel that this is a situation in which it would be permissible to protest against one's government.

They like to turn their study into action, and when they hear that a peace protest is being organized in central London, they start to make plans to join it. They will make banners, as they think it is important that Christians are seen to be active in campaigning for peace.

The peace march is, unfortunately, on a weekday. The school, hearing of their plans, says that if they take the day off school, it will be counted as truancy and will go on their reports to the universities to which they are applying.

Alice raises the subject in a roundabout way with her father and gets a blast of angry ridicule. Is that what comes of reading the Bible? He thought it said that you should honor your parents! It is an insult to his life's work, his inside information and superior judgment. What will his colleagues and friends think if they find out that his daughter is a peace protester? She is too old for him to ban her from going on a peace march if she wants to associate herself with "people like that," but he can insist that she comply with the school rules and the law of the land and not endanger the future that he has paid so much to provide for her.

Alice doesn't know what to do.

ALICE TURNS TO THE BIBLE

At their next study, the group is going to look at Philippians 4, so Alice gets her Bible out and reads it for herself.

I plead with Euodia and I plead with Syntyche to agree with each other in the Lord. Yes, and I ask you, loyal yokefellow, help these women who have contended at my side in the cause of the gospel, along with Clement and the rest of my fellow workers, whose names are in the book of life.

Rejoice in the Lord always. I will say it again: Rejoice! Let your gentleness be evident to all. The Lord is near. Do not be anxious about anything, but in everything, by prayer and petition, with thanksgiving, present your requests to God. And the peace of God, which transcends all understanding, will guard your hearts and your minds in Christ Jesus.

Finally, brothers, whatever is true, whatever is noble, whatever is right, whatever is pure, whatever is lovely, whatever is admirable—if anything is excellent or praiseworthy—think about such things. Whatever you have learned or received or heard from me, or seen in me—put it into practice. And the God of peace will be with you.

I rejoice greatly in the Lord that at last you have renewed your concern for me. Indeed, you have been concerned, but you had no opportunity to show it. I am not saying this because I am in need, for I have learned to be content whatever the circumstances. I know what it is to be in need, and I know what it is to have plenty. I have learned the secret of being content in any and every situation, whether well fed or hungry, whether living in plenty or in want. I can do everything through him who gives me strength. (Philippians 4:2–13)

THREE APPROACHES TO SOLVING THE PROBLEM

Looking for rules

Alice looks at the passage to see if it contains any clear directions that might help her to decide what to do. The passage seems full of commands: rejoice, let your gentleness show, don't be anxious, pray, be grateful, think about the right things, copy me! It seems to Alice, however, that these are not the sorts of things you can command. You can't be a joyful, gentle, confident, grateful, self-controlled person just because you are told to be. It doesn't work

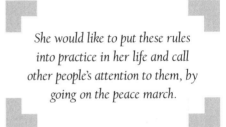

She would like to put these rules into practice in her life and call other people's attention to them, by going on the peace march.

like that. She needs to know what rules there are, if any, that lay down the circumstances in which war and civil disobedience are permitted for a Christian, and this passage doesn't seem to be any help with that.

Paul's advice that the Philippians let their "gentleness be evident to all" reminds Alice of the Sermon on the Mount, where Jesus says, "Blessed are the peacemakers, for they will be called sons of God" and tells his followers to love their enemies and turn the other cheek (Matthew 5:9, 39, 44). She would like to put these rules into practice in her life and call other people's attention to them, by going on the peace march.

Her father has already pointed out that one of the Ten Commandments says, "Honor your father and your mother" (Exodus 20:12). Paul also says in Romans 13 that Christians should give honor where it is due (v. 7) and, although some members of her study group questioned it, she was impressed by his insistence that everyone must submit themselves to the governing authorities (v. 1). By taking the day off school to go on the march, she would be defying her father, her school, and the government.

Alice's conclusion

With considerable resentment and frustration, Alice decides that although she is fairly sure it would be wrong for her country to go to war, and although she thinks it's important that she witness to the fact that God is a God of peace, she ought to abandon her friends on this occasion and look for some other way of registering her protest. She hopes they will understand.

LOOKING AT CONSEQUENCES

When Alice explains her thinking to the study group, one of the other girls says that Christians are not bound by rules anymore; they should let love decide what they do. She reminds Alice that Romans 13 continues, "Love is the fulfillment of the law" (v. 10). "Think of the consequences of what you do," the other girl says. "If you go on the march, your father will be angry and upset. You love him and this will make you sad, but imagine what will happen if the protest is so large that the government has to think again and decides not to go to war. You will then be saving thousands of people from violence, death, and homelessness, and from the results of escalating terror throughout the world. Do you love all those people as much as you love yourself? Are you prepared to pay the cost of upsetting your father and getting a black mark on your records, if you can stand up for love and peace in the world, let people see that Christians have something distinctive to say and are not afraid to say it?"

> *By taking the day off school to go on the march, she would be defying her father, her school, and the government.*

They look at the passage together and see from Paul's plea to Euodia and Syntyche that he expects Christians to be peacemakers. God is a "God of peace" and his people should be willing to testify to that without being anxious about the results of standing up for him. Alice should not concentrate her thoughts on the negative aspects—on her father's misguided belief that war achieves anything, or on the tension at home that might result from her action. She should think rather of the good things she might achieve in the world. She should do what she knows is right and put up with the "fallout" at home.

wrestling with life's tough issues

Alice's conclusion

Alice is swayed by her friend's argument that this is how she should approach the Bible passage and that the right thing for her to do in this situation is to join her friends on the march and take the consequences.

Some Christians may be concerned that although approaching the Bible in these two different ways has led to different actions, they have both resulted in a rather shallow and immature reading of the passage—what you might perhaps expect from young people of this age. A lot of what the passage teaches, which could lead to a more mature Christian approach to the situation, seems to have been missed.

LOOKING FOR VIRTUES

Let us suppose that a teacher joins the study group and, asking what they have been discussing, suggests that they look at Philippians 4 in another way, considering what virtues Paul is recommending to Christians. She challenges them to ask themselves how they can express and promote these virtues in their own lives, and particularly in their decision about whether or not to go on the peace march.

Alice will then be able to see that Paul is telling the members of the young church at Philippi how to find an inner peace in a troubled world—telling them that this can be done by developing a virtuous character, by pursuing and acquiring the virtues of joy, gentleness, confidence, gratitude, self-control, trust, and contentment. These are not feelings or actions that can be commanded, but they are virtues that can be sought and found in a lifelong task of growing in holiness.

Should she think rather of the good things she might achieve in the world? Should she do what she knows is right and put up with the "fallout" at home?

Alice sees that the passage starts with Paul pleading with two women in the church to agree with each other, to stop quarrelling. Christians should work at being amiable and avoid quarrels even if they don't hold the same opinions about everything.

She discovers that gentleness is a quality that Paul recommends here, not only for nations and governments but also for individuals. Alice begins to feel challenged about her hostility toward her father and their endless arguments.

Now that she is approaching adulthood, this is as much her responsibility as his. She will not find peace in herself if she cannot promote peace in her family and home. Perhaps she should listen to what he has to say about the war in Iraq and try to understand his perspective.

Don't be anxious

Alice then has to face her anxiety about living in London, which she feels may be one of the main reasons she so desperately doesn't want the country to go to war. If she can learn to trust God more by filling her prayers with gratitude and confident requests, maybe she can become a less anxious person, even if she does have to go on living in a world that is increasingly tense and dangerous.

The pictures of terrorist attacks that she has seen on television and in the newspapers fascinate and haunt her, and perhaps she needs to make a real effort to think about something else. She also likes, in quiet moments, to go over her arguments with her father in her head, tending her wounds and fantasizing about defeating and humiliating him. She is challenged to try to fill her mind with more peaceful and constructive thoughts.

Alice decides that in her present situation it is more appropriate for her to work at being a peacemaker at home, rather than a peacemaker on the streets of London.

Paul's emphasis on becoming a peaceful person does not diminish Alice's belief in a God of peace and the possibility—the urgency—of finding peaceful resolutions to the conflicts between nations, tribes, and cultures. It doesn't diminish her belief that as a responsible citizen she has the right and the duty to communicate this feeling in some way to a government on the brink of war, but the passage also challenges her at a personal level. God has promised that an inner peace is part of the fruit of his Spirit's work in us (Galatians 5:22). If she lets him in and works with him, he can change her from the restless, quarrelsome, and anxious person that she is now.

Alice's conclusion

Alice decides that in her present situation it is more appropriate for her to work at being a peacemaker at home, rather than a peacemaker on the streets of London. At this stage of her life, being a good daughter is at least as important as being a good citizen. She will soon be leaving and will become more independent of her parents. Things will be different then, but while she is living with them, it is appropriate for her to express her love for them by honoring them in this way. She can find other ways of protesting about the war.

Peace

Seeing peace as a virtue—an inward feature of character that predisposes someone to feel and think and act in certain ways—helped Alice in the last chapter to engage with Paul's teaching on peace. The passage helped them to resolve a particular dilemma and move forward in Christian maturity. But can approaching this passage, and the New Testament concept of peace, in this way be justified independently of this particular story?

Peace is a rich concept throughout the Bible. It describes a state of completion, soundness, and well-being in and between people, communities, and God. In 1 Kings 5:12 we read that there were "peaceful relations" between King Solomon and one of his neighbors and they expressed this peace with a treaty. Psalm 122:6–7 calls people to pray for the peace of Jerusalem: "May those who love you be secure. May there be peace within your walls and security within your citadels." Jeremiah

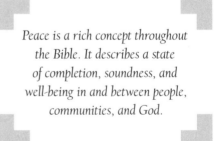

Peace is a rich concept throughout the Bible. It describes a state of completion, soundness, and well-being in and between people, communities, and God.

tells the exiles to "seek the peace and prosperity of the city to which I have carried you" (Jeremiah 29:7), and in Psalm 4:8 the psalmist says, "I will lie down and sleep in peace, for you alone, O Lord, make me dwell in safety."

PEACE, WISDOM, AND RIGHTEOUSNESS

In the Bible, peace, for individuals and for communities, is intimately connected with wisdom and with righteousness. Proverbs 3:17 tells us that wisdom's ways "are pleasant ways, and all her paths are peace." In Isaiah we read, "The fruit of righteousness will be peace; the effect of righteousness will be quietness and confidence forever" (32:17), and God will keep "in perfect peace" those whose minds are steadfast, because they trust in him (26:3). "There is no peace,' says my God, 'for the wicked'" (57:21).

The new age that the Messiah, the "Prince of Peace," will bring in will be an age of "justice and righteousness" (Isaiah 9:6–7). Zion's new king "will proclaim peace to the nations" (Zechariah 9:10).

The New Testament claims these prophecies for Jesus. Another Zechariah, John the Baptist's father, declares that the infant Jesus will "guide our feet into the path of peace" (Luke 1:79), and the angels sing, "Glory to God in the highest, and on earth peace to men on whom his favor rests" (Luke 2:14).

For the period of time between his first coming as Savior and his return as judge at the end of time, however, Jesus rather changes the focus. He says, "Do you think I came to bring peace on earth? No, I tell you, but division" (Luke 12:51). Jesus does give his peace to his followers, but it is "not . . . as the world gives" it. He tells them not to let their hearts be troubled and not to be afraid (John 14:27). "In the world you will have trouble," he says. "But take heart! I have overcome the world" (John 16:33). For the time being, Christians are not promised a peaceful environment, but they are given a gift of inner peace, which they are called to develop and express—as peacemakers—in a world full of conflict, tension, and alarm.

The gospel of peace

The focus of Paul's gospel is that Christ has opened a way for us to find peace with God (Romans 5:1). Jesus reconciles everything to God "by making peace through his blood, shed on the cross" (Colossians 1:20).

Paul then makes his customary logical move from the facts of the gospel to the implications for how Christians ought to live. He urges us not only to make peace with God and to pray for peace in the world (1 Timothy 2:2) but also to make peace with others: "If it is possible, as far as it depends on you, live at peace with everyone" (Romans 12:18). Christians are to avoid dissension and quarrelling (Romans 13:13; 2 Corinthians 12:20), and to cooperate with the Spirit as he grows his fruit of peace in them (Galatians 5:22). The church community is to be a foretaste of God's peaceful kingdom (Ephesians 2:14–16; 4:3), and Paul urges the Colossians to "Let the peace of Christ rule in your hearts, since as members of one body you were called to peace" (Colossians 3:15). Peter, in his first letter, tells Christians to "live in harmony with one another," to "seek peace and pursue it" (1 Peter 3:8, 11).

Peace is, then, not only an external state of affairs between people, nations, and God that we should pray and work for, but also an inner state—one of the virtues that Christians are called to pursue. This is borne out by its connection with all the other virtues—with righteousness. We saw in Philippians 4 (Alice's reading) that Paul instructed the church to avoid quarrelsomeness, to be peacemakers, to hold on to joy, to cultivate gentleness, to overcome anxiety, to pray with gratitude, to learn to trust, to put their attention in the right place, to pursue contentment—and then, says Paul, "the peace of God, which transcends all understanding, will guard your hearts and your minds in Christ Jesus" (4:7).

Peace is, then, not only an external state of affairs between people, nations, and God that we should pray and work for, but also an inner state—one of the virtues that Christians are called to pursue.

Coming to this topic from a Virtue Ethics perspective helps us to understand more clearly how Paul sees Christian growth toward maturity and holiness. We grow not by struggling to keep rules or calculate consequences but by responding to what God has done for us, and by pursuing the virtue of love as it is modeled to us by Jesus—a love that is filled out with all the other Christian virtues and turned into action with a godly wisdom. Paul believes that God can change not only our behavior but also our nature, so that we become amiable, joyful, gentle, confident, grateful, self-controlled, contented, and peaceful people.

PRACTICAL WISDOM

Knowing how to balance and apply these virtues to specific situations requires the practical wisdom that both Virtue Ethics and the New Testament associate with peace, for some external situations require peaceful solutions and some call for peace not to be the overriding concern. When Jesus was arrested in the garden of Gethsemane, he rebuked one of his companions for turning to violence: "Put your sword back in its place," Jesus told him, "for all who draw the sword will die by the sword" (Matthew 26:52). But when confronted by the traders and money changers in the temple, Jesus made a whip, overturned their tables, and drove them out, saying, "Get these out of here! How dare you turn my Father's house into a market!" (John 2:14–16).

An inappropriate expression of peace can, if too little emphasis is put upon it for the particular situation, become the vice of hostility and aggression. If it receives too much emphasis in another situation, it can become the vice of cowardice and complacency. No universal rule tells us that we should always take the most peaceful option or that a forceful response is permitted in this or that specified circumstance.

Old Testament wisdom teaches, "There is a time for everything, and a season for every activity under heaven. . . . A time to kill and a time to heal, a time to tear down and a time to build . . . a time to be silent and a time to speak . . . a time for war and a time for peace" (Ecclesiastes 3:1, 3, 7–8). It is the virtuous—the righteous and the wise—who can live like this, and this is the life to which the New Testament calls us to aspire.

Loving ourselves

Peace is called a "self-regarding" virtue by some philosophers interested in Virtue Ethics. Being at peace with God and with ourselves does not primarily control how we think, feel, and act toward other people, in the way that virtues like kindness, honesty, gentleness, and justice do. It controls how we think and feel about ourselves and our place in the world. As we have already seen, a number of the most prominent Christian virtues come into this category. Developing peace, joy, hope, moderation, courage, perseverance, and contentment does not directly benefit other people but benefits the person who acquires them—although we all know that people who have these virtues are, on the whole, more pleasant and more uplifting to be with. They represent something of what the Bible shows as human life reaching its potential, the life to the full that Jesus came to bring to the world (John 10:10).

The ethics of rules and the ethics of consequences have been criticized by some philosophers for having a kind of asymmetry.[36] While we have a duty to avoid dishonesty, injustice, and harm in our dealings with other people, saving ourselves from pain and pursuing our own happiness are, according to Kant's ethics, merely permitted. In the ethics of consequences, the self-regarding virtues also seem to be neglected. It is the other-regarding virtue of benevolence that takes center stage: we must always be prepared to sacrifice our own happiness and the happiness of those close to us for the sake of the greater good, even the good of strangers. In spite of claiming to believe in

wrestling with life's tough issues

the equal value of every person, in both these approaches the value of the self seems to disappear.

By contrast, Virtue Ethics and New Testament ethics emphasize both self-regarding virtues and the special responsibilities incurred in certain kinds of relationships. This helps to resolve a long-standing disagreement among Christians about what Jesus meant when he said, "Love your neighbor as yourself." Did he mean, "Love both your neighbor and yourself," or "Love your neighbor as much as you (inevitably) love yourself," or "Love your neighbor instead of loving yourself"?

There is a strong Christian tradition which says that he meant the last of these options. The argument is that Christian love is essentially selfless love and so it can't be turned in on the self. Luther, for example, believed that self-love was the very essence of sin.[37] This argument is in line with the ethical systems of Kant and Mill, but

> *Virtue Ethics and New Testament ethics emphasize both self-regarding virtues and the special responsibilities incurred in certain kinds of relationships.*

Virtue Ethics takes a rather different perspective: acquiring the virtues—becoming a virtuous person—is seen to benefit the self, while the value of the self, its well-being and interests, is one important factor in the resolution of moral dilemmas. The New Testament's emphasis on self-regarding virtues would seem to reflect this approach.

Neither Kant's assumption that everyone loves themselves inevitably and spontaneously, and will always put their own welfare first, nor Mill's assumption that everyone's happiness counts equally in the calculation of right actions, are taken for granted by Virtue Ethics and the New Testament. There is no rule in Scripture that says, "You shall not love yourself." We are called to love ourselves in the right way and to avoid loving ourselves in the wrong way. Seeing self-love as a virtue captures this calling. Learning to apply this virtue wisely helps us to avoid both the vices of self-centeredness and inappropriate self-assertion and the vices of self-deprecation and inappropriate self-neglect.

Because of this emphasis, Virtue Ethics has sometimes been criticized for encouraging a selfish approach to moral living: I look inward and work at developing my own character so that I can have a flourishing life. In fact, however, Aristotle was convinced that individuals flourish only in flourishing communities, within healthy, creative, and mutually benefiting networks of relationships. This means that the inward-looking virtues—contentment, purity, self-control, peace, and so on—can grow only alongside the outward-looking virtues, such

peace

as benevolence, empathy, generosity, honesty, and so on. The New Testament mirrors this emphasis on the quality of communities as well as individuals.

OVERCOMING THE EGO

Jesus' teaching on self-denial (Mark 8:34–35; John 15:13; Luke 14:26–27) and Paul's teaching to regard the body as the temple of the Holy Spirit (1 Corinthians 6:19) can, then, both be understood in the right way. The ethical task of overcoming the ego has to start from an acceptance and valuing of the ego. We cannot give our self away unless we first possess it, and this is exactly where the gospel of Jesus starts.

We begin to receive his forgiveness and healing, to find peace with God. The gift of his sanctifying Spirit enables us to develop the virtue of peace.

The story of Jesus' death and resurrection for us enables us to believe in his love, his acceptance of us as we are. We begin to receive his forgiveness and healing, to find peace with God. The gift of his sanctifying Spirit enables us to develop the virtue of peace—an inner state of contentment and confidence that enhances our lives, helping us to live life to the full, to start overcoming the inappropriate demands of a restless ego and so to act lovingly and wisely toward others. This is the ethics of the New Testament, which the rediscovery of the ethics of virtue in the philosophical world can help us to recapture.

wrestling with life's tough issues

14

Patricia and Timothy receive an unexpected inheritance and look at 2 Corinthians 8 and 9

PATRICIA AND TIMOTHY'S STORY

Timothy is an engineer working for a large firm of building consultants. His wife Patricia returned to full-time teaching once their youngest child started school, and now that all their children have left home, Patricia and Timothy are enjoying a comfortable lifestyle (though not, in their estimation, an extravagant one). They are both paying into pension plans and feel secure about their future, although they have accepted that when they are both retired, their income will drop quite significantly.

Then Patricia's aunt dies and leaves her an unexpectedly large inheritance. The couple were not aware that the aunt had that much money, and now there are decisions to make about what to do with it.

They both think it would be wise to put some of this money away for the future, but Timothy would like to spend some of it now—on an expensive car. He argues that they have always economized by buying small, second-hand cars, and he would love, just once in his life, to buy a good new car that will last him into his retirement. Patricia replies that she would like a new kitchen. There is nothing wrong with the old one, but it looks shabby and old-fashioned compared with the kitchen that their daughter has in her new house. In addition, most of their vacations with the children were spent camping, and they agree that it would be wonderful to go to Italy together, to see Rome, Florence, and Venice.

They both give to their local church on a regular basis, using their bank's automatic withdrawal system, and they are sometimes moved to give to national appeals for world disasters. The idea of giving some of their inheritance away does not occur to them until, one Sunday morning, the preacher gives a sermon about giving, taken from some passages in 2 Corinthians. On the way home from church, they both admit that they have been challenged by what they have heard.

Patricia and Timothy turn to the Bible

At lunch, Timothy suggests that they look for themselves at the Bible passages they heard in church that morning and think again about the money they have inherited. They read this:

> And now, brothers, we want you to know about the grace that God has given the Macedonian churches. Out of the most severe trial, their overflowing joy and their extreme poverty welled up in rich generosity. For I testify that they gave as much as they were able, and even beyond their ability. Entirely on their own, they urgently pleaded with us for the privilege of sharing in this service to the saints. And they did not do as we expected, but they gave themselves first to the Lord and then to us in keeping with God's will. . . . But just as you excel in everything—in faith, in speech, in knowledge, in complete earnestness and in your love for us—see that you also excel in this grace of giving. . . .
>
> For you know the grace of our Lord Jesus Christ, that though he was rich, yet for your sakes he became poor, so that you through his poverty might become rich. . . .
>
> For if the willingness is there, the gift is acceptable according to what one has, not according to what he does not have.
>
> Our desire is not that others might be relieved while you are hard pressed, but that there might be equality. At the present time your plenty will supply what they need, so that in turn their plenty will supply what you need. Then there will be equality. . . .
>
> Remember this: Whoever sows sparingly will also reap sparingly, and whoever sows generously will also reap generously. Each man should give what he has decided in his heart to give, not reluctantly or under compulsion, for God loves a cheerful giver. And God is able to make all grace abound to you, so that in all things at all times, having all that you need, you will abound in every good work. . . . You will be made rich in every way so that you can be generous on every occasion, and through us your generosity will result in thanksgiving to God.
>
> This service that you perform is not only supplying the needs of God's people but is also overflowing in many expressions of thanks to God. Because of

wrestling with life's tough issues

the service by which you have proved yourselves, men will praise God for the obedience that accompanies your confession of the gospel of Christ, and for your generosity in sharing with them and with everyone else. And in their prayers for you their hearts will go out to you, because of the surpassing grace God has given you. Thanks be to God for his indescribable gift! (2 Corinthians 8:1–5, 7, 9, 12–14; 9:6–8, 11–15)

THREE APPROACHES TO SOLVING THE PROBLEM

LOOKING FOR RULES

Timothy, who thinks that you know where you are with rules, has always had in the back of his mind the Old Testament rules about tithing. Seeing Paul's reference to "the obedience that accompanies the gospel," he thinks that this must mean obedience to those laws. He remembers his Sunday school classes, where he was introduced to the principle of giving 10 percent of our income to God, and is pleased to reflect on the fact that he has followed this rule, more or less, since then—except during the years when Patricia wasn't working, the mortgage was enormous, and finances were a bit tight.

Timothy suggests that they look for themselves at the Bible passages they heard in church that morning and think again about the money they have inherited.

Timothy gets out some commentaries and discovers that the laws of tithing were actually quite complicated, but he likes Leviticus 27:30, which says quite plainly, "A tithe of everything from the land, whether grain from the soil or fruit from the trees, belongs to the Lord; it is holy to the Lord." He feels that the salary he receives from his daily work is comparable to the produce from a farmer's land, and, since the tithe in Old Testament times was clearly a kind of tax, he has always calculated 10 percent of his income after tax to the government and the local authority has been paid.

Timothy isn't sure, however, that an inheritance counts as income in the same way. He can't imagine that a son inheriting his father's estate in Old Testament times would have been required to pay a tithe on that. He and Patricia are not inheriting a piece of land or a business, just some money, so he decides that realistically it does count as income for them.

Their church has an ongoing fund to repay a debt incurred when the roof had to be repaired urgently a few years ago. Timothy feels bad that he hasn't thought of it before, but a substantial one-off payment from their inheritance to the fund would make a big dent in the church's remaining debt and fulfill the obligations of Christian giving.

Timothy's conclusion

Timothy tells Patricia that he has thought it through and decided that their inheritance should count as income. He believes that 10 percent of it therefore belongs to God, so they should give it to the church debt fund. There will still be enough left for a reasonable car and a less expensive vacation and some money to save for their retirement.

LOOKING AT CONSEQUENCES

Patricia asks him if he has listened to the sermon or looked at the passage from 2 Corinthians at all! The people Paul was writing to there were probably already paying taxes to the Romans and giving to their own churches. They were responding to a particular situation: "supplying the needs of God's people" (9:12). This is not about keeping rules but a response of love. It is about making a difference to the lives of people you care about.

Patricia reminds Timothy of what they heard in the sermon about the famine in Judea and Paul's desire that the Gentile churches should show their concern for and unity with Jewish Christians who were having a particularly bad time. They weren't calculating percentages of their income and giving it to their own church; they were looking beyond their obligations to God and their own community to the urgent needs of fellow Christians of another race and continent, whom they had never met. They were following the example of Jesus, who gave up everything to save us, and were giving "beyond their ability" (8:3).

> *Timothy tells Patricia that he has thought it through and decided that their inheritance should count as income. He believes that 10 percent of it therefore belongs to God.*

Patricia remembers, from the Gospels, how Jesus criticized the Pharisees for tithing their spices and neglecting the more important matters of the law—justice, mercy, and faithfulness (Matthew 23:23)—and how he commended the poor widow who, out of her poverty, put everything she had in the temple treasury (Mark 12:44).

"Giving isn't for our sake," she tells Timothy, "so that we feel good about having fulfilled our obligations; it's for the sake of people in need. We have to think about the consequences, not the rules—the real difference we will be making to other people's lives."

When she looks again at 2 Corinthians, she discovers what Paul says should be the consequences of our giving: that there should be equality between those with more than they need and those with less. Patricia is immediately reminded of the story of Jesus and the rich ruler in Luke 18. Jesus told him to sell everything he had and give to the poor. Then, he said, "you will have treasure in heaven" (v. 22).

Let us love one another with actions

The preacher had mentioned in her sermon a passage from one of John's letters: "This is how we know what love is: Jesus Christ laid down his life for us. And we ought to lay down our lives for our brothers. If anyone has material possessions and sees his brother in need but has no pity on him, how can the love of God be in him? Dear children, let us not love with words or tongue but with actions and in truth" (1 John 3:16–18).

Patricia does feel pity for the people suffering from extreme poverty that she sees on her television screen. "If we're going to live by what the Bible says," she tells Timothy, "we should get rid of the world's idea that what we have and what we earn is for ourselves, to give us more secure, comfortable, and rich lives. Ten percent is nothing if we still have so much more than we need while others are destitute. The more we give, the better the consequences, so we should go on giving and not stop until there is an equality of living standards for people all around the world."

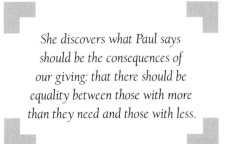

She discovers what Paul says should be the consequences of our giving: that there should be equality between those with more than they need and those with less.

Patricia's conclusion

Even as she says it, Patricia realizes the real implication: that they should give away not only all their inheritance but all their savings, their pension fund, and most of their possessions. They could still get what they need to stay alive from their state pensions. Then she sees that even if they gave everything, although this might keep a few children alive or give one family or one village a better life, it would hardly change the situation of inequality in the world at all. The developed world would still be stifled with affluence and the developing world dying of destitution. If we look at what our giving actually achieves, it is very depressing. "It would be better to give it all to one of those organizations that work for free trade and world justice," she adds as an afterthought. "It might do more good there."

They begin to aspire to develop this virtue and can see from the Bible passage that it grows from recognizing God's amazing generosity to us.

"But we're not going to do that, are we?" Timothy replies, and Patricia says, "I don't really think God is asking us to do that."

LOOKING FOR VIRTUES

Approaching this Bible passage from these two different perspectives has led to two different outcomes for Timothy and Patricia in this situation. Although Paul does talk about the "obedience" that accompanies the confession of the gospel, his exhortation to the Corinthian church about giving doesn't seem to be captured at all by Timothy's "rules" approach, and looking at giving from the perspective of consequences has led Patricia to an unrealistic and ultimately depressing conclusion.

Gratitude and generosity

Let us imagine that Patricia and Timothy come to the passage not looking for rules to keep or at the consequences of their actions but, rather, looking for virtues. They will then see that the Christian virtues recommended here are gratitude and generosity. Paul is urging his readers not just to keep some rules, or just to act in order to help their fellow Christians, but to become more generous people in response to what they have experienced of God's generosity.

Reading the passage like this makes Patricia realize that although she has given to the church and to charities all her life, she has done so with a rather selfish spirit. She resented it quite strongly when Timothy returned to tithing their joint income when she restarted work, feeling that all of her earnings should have been for her to spend on what she wanted. She has responded to national appeals from time to time but that was mostly, she realizes now, to make herself feel better about the awful pictures in the media. In 2 Corinthians, Christian giving doesn't seem to be like that at all. Paul thought that God's "indescribable gift" and Jesus' complete giving of himself for us should stir in us a response—a grateful and gracious acceptance of all that we have as a gift from God, and a cheerful willingness to respect it and share our enjoyment of it with other people, especially if their need is greater than ours.

The giving of the Macedonian church, as Paul describes it, didn't come only from a sense of duty or a desire to change the world: their joy at being recipients of God's grace in Jesus "welled up in rich generosity" (8:2), and they gave not just their money but themselves to God and to the Christian community. Their giving to their fellow Christians in Judea just seemed to flow from their understanding of the gospel story in a natural and joyful way.

Patricia and Timothy have some friends who, as they have commented recently, are just generous people. They are generous with their time and their home, generous with their possessions, their thoughts, and their words. These friends don't think of 10 percent of their income as belonging to God, but seem to receive everything with gratitude as a gift from him and get real enjoyment from it as they celebrate and share it with anyone and everyone. As Paul says in 2 Corinthians, their lives do seem "rich in every way" (9:11).

In comparison, Patricia and Timothy's lives seem quite stingy. After fulfilling what they see as their Christian duty to give, they have guarded and cherished their time and their possessions as their own and judged other people uncharitably. With a different attitude, they could host the house group sometimes, even if it might spoil the new carpet. They could use their car for giving lifts to the elderly, lend their books and tools, and let their nephew stay when he comes to London for meetings. They could be more forgiving to the noisy teenagers next door and make more of an effort to spend time with Timothy's mother. All these things seem to them to flow from the virtue of generosity.

Developing generosity

They begin to aspire to develop this virtue and can see from the Bible passage that it grows from recognizing God's amazing generosity to us. Timothy points out the role that regular, engaged worship can have in developing the virtue of gratitude, especially the Communion service, where they remember what Jesus has done for them and receive God's gracious gifts from him.

Returning to 2 Corinthians, they see that the Macedonians' generosity overflowed into giving to fellow Christians in other parts of the world who were having a hard time, in order to express unity and care for them. Timothy and Patricia's church supports an aid worker who is trying to help people return from a refugee camp and begin farming again. Patricia says that this is the sort of thing she would like to get more involved in. Timothy adds that, as well as giving to this project, they could perhaps even visit, after they have retired, and offer some practical help.

Timothy and Patricia's conclusion

Studying this passage of the Bible together and discovering the Christian virtues of gratitude and generosity lead Timothy and Patricia to decide to spend some time reflecting on their life—what they do with their time and their income and how they feel about their possessions, their retirement, and their inheritance—in the light of their faith in God as their creator and the story of Jesus' life and death for them.

It seems amazing that, in so many years of churchgoing, they have never done this before. They have never thought through how their daily lives could reflect their faith in a generous creator of a good world, who asks us to respect and care for it, and their faith in a generous savior who lived and died for others and calls his followers to do the same. They have never taken on board the Bible's repeated warnings about the spiritual dangers

They begin to see that their lives will be happier and more authentic if they are simpler, less wasteful, and more generous.

of having more than enough of the world's good things (see, for example, Deuteronomy 8:10–14; Luke 12:16–21; 1 Timothy 6:10; James 5:1–6). They begin to see that their lives will be happier and more authentic if they are simpler, less wasteful, and more generous.

Whether or not they decide to get a new car or do some home improvements, they can immediately offer to use their car for taking people to church and open their home more for entertaining.

Because Paul says that the Corinthians should make a conscious decision about how much they give away, Patricia and Timothy decide to put 10 percent of their inheritance in a separate bank account so that it is earmarked for giving away. They then start praying that God will lead them to some charities, Christian work, or a project they can get involved in that will express their gratitude to God for all his goodness to them, and their care for the world he has made.

Grace

THE SUBJECT OF CHRISTIAN GIVING can be approached from the perspective of rules, consequences, or Virtue Ethics. As we saw in the last chapter, these different approaches lead people to different thoughts and actions, and each one has its advantages.

At one level, giving is a matter of obedience for Christians, and, as Paul suggests, it is good for it to be an organized habit rather than a random response (see 1 Corinthians 16:2). Rules about giving in the Bible seem mostly to point to giving away 10 percent of our income, and this is a great deal more than most Christians give away today.

A "consequences" approach highlights feelings of compassion for those in need, which is clearly part of Christian giving (see 1 John 3:17), but if we are only motivated by a desire to see good results from our giving, we can become rather overwhelmed and therefore paralyzed, particularly as we experience the world today. The popularity of raffles in church fund-raising and of sponsoring individual children in the underdeveloped world, even when most aid organizations would rather help whole communities, is perhaps a reflection of this desire to see good consequences from our giving.

GRACE AT THE HEART OF THE GOSPEL

Can Virtue Ethics incorporate these insights and add anything new to the subject of Christian giving? As we have seen in the previous chapter, a Virtue Ethics approach to Christian giving highlights the virtue of generosity, which Christians know as grace—the liberality and mercy of God to the undeserving. God creates and saves and gives and forgives, taking risks and making himself vulnerable, just because it is his nature to do so, and he calls his followers to become like him. This approach reveals to us not only that love must be the motivation of Christian giving, but also the special nature of that love, and how it can be developed and expressed. It reminds us that we are both justified and sanctified by grace and that the hallmark of God's kingdom is the virtue of generosity.

A Virtue Ethics approach to Christian giving brings the subject back from years of neglect to where it should be, where it is in the Gospels: right at the center of Christian ethics. The lives of Christians should, above everything else, reflect the generosity of God. A Virtue Ethics approach also reminds us that the love at the heart of Christian ethics is a certain kind of love: it is given irrespective of the qualities of the recipient, and with no ulterior motive. It is a love that gives itself, and goes on giving and forgiving without consideration of the returns, risks, or consequences. It encapsulates the virtues of mercy, kindness, pity, charity, patience, forbearance, hospitality, and faithfulness, but it is best captured in the virtue of generosity.

> *A Virtue Ethics approach to Christian giving highlights the virtue of generosity, which Christians know as grace—the liberality and mercy of God to the undeserving.*

Whether or not this insight into Christian ethics is reflected in the teaching of the New Testament can be demonstrated by looking at some examples of Jesus' teaching in Matthew's Gospel.

God's generosity in creation is indiscriminate (Matthew 5:43–48)

When Jesus tells his followers to love their enemies, it is because they will then be children of their Father in heaven, sharing in his character. God's character is shown in that "He causes his sun to rise on the evil and the good, and sends rain on the righteous and the unrighteous" (v. 45). Don't love those who are loveable in order to get loved in return, Jesus tells his followers; everyone does that. You must be perfect—like your heavenly Father.

God creates and sustains his creation with a generous love and pours his gifts and blessings indiscriminately on all his creatures, not picking favorites or rewarding service or looking for returns, but just because it is his nature to give. Jesus urges his followers to respond to this generosity by becoming generous people themselves.

Seeing God's creation as a gift of grace is a motivation for much more than giving away 10 percent of our income. It is the root of a grateful spirit that lifts us into worship, and also of a sense of responsibility for the development and preservation of the natural world.

Generosity does not look for anything in return (Matthew 6:1)

Jesus tells his followers not to give in order to be seen and admired, but to give in secret so that only God knows what they are doing. Those who are rewarded by seeing the results of their giving do not receive the hidden rewards of truly godly giving.

God's generosity is prodigal and risky (Matthew 13:1–23)

God's giving is not calculated for maximum results but, like the sower in biblical times, his word is spread abroad with the acceptance that much of it may not directly achieve anything at all. Our giving should reflect the fact that God gives in such a prodigal and risky way, not driven by careful calculation of results. This does not mean that we should be unwise in our giving, just that it should contain no hint of meanness or self-interest.

God's hospitality is open-handed (Matthew 22:1–10)

The picture of God's salvation as a banquet, a party, often a wedding, is one that occurs in both Old and New Testaments (see, for example, Isaiah 25:6–8; Revelation 19:6–8) and appears frequently in Jesus' stories of the kingdom. It illustrates God's open-handed hospitality. In the story in Matthew 22, those invited cannot be bothered to attend, so the king's servants are instructed to go to the 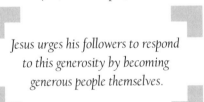 *Jesus urges his followers to respond to this generosity by becoming generous people themselves.* street corners and invite anyone they find, good and bad. In the version told by Luke, the king tells his servants, "Go out to the roads and country lanes and make them come in, so that my house will be full," and adds, "I tell you, not one of those men who were invited will get a taste of my banquet" (Luke 14:23–24). Again we see a picture of God as one whose generous nature makes it imperative that he throw a party and that his table be full. Any and all of those who discover and are able to receive this generosity find his salvation.

God's grace does not calculate what we deserve (Matthew 20:1–16)

"Are you envious because I am generous?" is the closing question that the landowner puts to the workers in his vineyard who think they have been treated unfairly (v. 15). Those who started work at dawn have received what they were promised, but those who only worked for one hour have received the same amount, and this doesn't seem fair.

The fact is that justice is not going to get anyone very far when it comes to receiving the gifts of God's salvation. Justice is about giving people what they are owed, but God's giving is not like that. Generosity means giving beyond what anyone expects or has any right to, giving with no thought about what the giver gets out of it or about what comes back in thanks or advantage. This is so foreign to the way people normally behave that we are shocked by this parable. We are shocked by the landowner's uncalled for, seemingly pointless generosity. This is, however, what we ourselves depend on if we are to receive God's gift of salvation. The story challenges us not to be envious or resentful of God's generosity to others but to be generous too—with our forgiveness, our acceptance of apologies, our evaluation of other people's worth, and our readiness to attribute sincerity and godliness to those who disagree with us, as well as with our skills, our income, and our possessions.

Blessed are the merciful (Matthew 5:7)

In his list of the character traits of those who find God and the gifts of his salvation, Jesus includes mercy. People who have the ability to be generous with the faults of others will, he tells us, receive the mercy of God.

Giving and receiving grace go hand in hand (Matthew 6:14)

Jesus repeats this teaching when, having told his followers to ask God for forgiveness, he points out the connection between giving and receiving grace. Developing a grateful and generous nature is the natural response to discovering and receiving God's grace, but it is also, it seems, a necessary response. The mean-spirited not only fail to show grace to others, but their ability to receive grace withers too.

The dynamics of generosity (Matthew 18:21–35)

Jesus makes a similar point with a story. The absurdity of a man being forgiven an enormous debt by the king and then demanding the payment of a tiny debt by his own servant helps us to see the dynamics of the virtue of generosity, the power of grace to transform our character, and the upward spiral of receiving and giving grace which living with God is all about. It shows us dramatically how central the virtue of generosity is to Christian ethics. It shows us why the merciful are blessed and why those who choose

wrestling with life's tough issues

the downward spiral of ingratitude and meanness fail to receive the blessings of God's salvation. It reminds us of the power of Communion to open our hearts to God's grace and so to nurture the virtues of gratitude and generosity within us.

Freely you have received, freely give (Matthew 10:8)

Among Jesus' instructions to the disciples when he sent them out to preach the gospel were the simple words, "Freely you have received, freely give."

Generosity is more important than the whole law (Matthew 19:16–30)

The story of Jesus' meeting with the "rich young man" makes a similar point. After the man has claimed that he has kept all the laws that relate to our relationships with one another, Jesus tells him that one more thing is necessary. If he wants to be a follower of Jesus, he must be willing to sell everything he has and give to the poor. The main stumbling block to this man's discovery of God was his "great wealth" (v. 22), which was stifling his ability to develop generosity and so both to give and receive grace.

Jesus goes on to explain the point more clearly when he says that it is easier for a camel to go through the eye of a needle than for a rich man to enter the kingdom of God (v. 24). The Bible is full of warnings about the spiritual dangers of affluence (see, for example, Deuteronomy 8:10–14; Isaiah 58:6–9; Luke 12:16–21; 1 Timothy 6:10; James 5:1–6), and it appears that wealth is dangerous because it breaks the connection between grace, gratitude, and generosity. The affluent easily forget that God is generous. They then develop difficulty with both showing generosity to others and receiving grace from God.

> *Christian giving, for many, has either become a matter of merely giving away a proportion of our income as a duty or has concentrated our attention on the results of our giving.*

Living for others is the secret of a fulfilling and authentic life (Matthew 10:39)

Jesus has been warning his hearers of how much he demands and how hard it can be to follow him. He talks of being willing to take up a cross, to lay down our life, if we are to be worthy of him, and then adds this enigmatic phrase: "Whoever finds his life will lose it, and whoever loses his life for my sake will find it." This is the peak of generosity, that we follow Jesus' example and are willing to give away all that we are and all that we have for the sake of others. A life lived generously—lived for others—is fulfilling and authentic. A life lived selfishly—holding on to our time and our possessions as if they belonged exclusively to us—is a life wasted and ultimately lost.

We are judged on our generosity to others (Matthew 25:31–46)

Jesus told another story that brings the idea of living a generous life to the center of his gospel, for it is the people who have fed the hungry, given water to the thirsty, taken in the stranger, clothed the poor, and visited the sick and the imprisoned that, in this story, enter into the kingdom. This can be hard to fit in with other ideas about being saved by grace rather than works, unless we consider the connection between grace, gratitude, and generosity that Virtue Ethics approaches remind us of so clearly.

THE VIRTUE OF GENEROSITY AT THE CENTER OF THE GOSPEL

These few examples from one of the Gospels confirm the absolute centrality of the virtue of generosity to Christian living. Many years of approaching ethics either looking for rules to keep or for consequences to calculate have contributed to the neglect of this fact among Christians. Christian giving, for many, has either become a matter of merely giving away a proportion of our income as a duty or has concentrated our attention on the results of our giving.

> *The insight of Virtue Ethics has revealed that the primary task of Christian living is to live in grace, letting God's Spirit develop this virtue of generosity in us.*

Approaching the subject of Christian giving from a Virtue Ethics perspective helps us to see that many of the Gospel stories and much of Paul's teaching present it in an altogether larger way. The discovery of God's generosity and the ability to receive it and show the same sort of generosity to others is at the very heart of the gospel. This compels Christians to reflect on their attitudes to their income and their possessions, their purchasing, saving, consumption, and waste, as well as their giving to relieve the hardship of the poor. It also compels them to reflect on their attitudes to their fellow human beings—their readiness to accept, to think the best, to keep on forgiving, as well as their attitude to sharing the good gifts they have received from God.

As Paul says in 1 Corinthians 13, the love of God, the love that the Holy Spirit longs to grow in us, is patient and kind. "It does not envy, it does not boast, it is not proud. It is not rude, it is not self-seeking, it is not easily angered, it keeps no record of wrongs. Love does not delight in evil but rejoices with the truth. It always protects, always trusts, always hopes, always perseveres" (vv. 4–7). This is Christian grace. The insight of Virtue Ethics has revealed that the primary task of Christian living is to live in grace, letting God's Spirit develop this virtue of generosity in us.

Section 3

Virtue Ethics evaluated

An introduction to the evaluation

THE CENTRAL SECTION OF THIS book explored how ordinary Christian people might go about making moral decisions and some of the different ways in which the Bible can be used to inspire and guide them toward acting with righteousness and pursuing inner holiness. I believe that turning away from the philosophical assumptions of the Enlightenment, which are in many ways alien to the biblical worldview, and turning toward an older philosophical system, which was familiar to the writers of the New Testament documents, has enabled us to see the ethical teaching in these documents in a new way, as a clear, coherent, and distinctive way of living.

This old philosophical approach, now known as Virtue Ethics, has been shown to be practically useful for individuals trying to interpret specific Bible passages, understand some of the key aspects of New Testament teaching on moral living, and make good choices in the complicated situations in which they find themselves.

In this last section, we will look at the usefulness of this approach not just to individuals wanting to mold their lives by the Bible but to Christians wanting to influence the democratic processes of lawmaking and to pursue peace and unity in the Church and in the world.

A great deal of public discussion about ethics is not about individual decisions like the ones covered in the central section of this book, but about making laws and setting values for societies. This process raises questions like "Should euthanasia be made legal?" "Should our country go to war?" "How should we treat asylum seekers or contribute to the development of poorer countries?"

These are rather different questions. You do not, for example, have to believe that suicide is always wrong to believe that it would be a mistake to legalize euthanasia. You can reasonably believe both that marriage is for life and that it is right for legal divorces to be available. You can appreciate both that the Bible's wisdom is a valuable asset to discussions about how to organize any society and that particular ways of behaving that are right for Christians should not be imposed by law on people who do not follow that religion. The first chapter in this section will look at how a Virtue Ethics approach can be used in wise legislation and how it might help Christians to make a more cohesive, and more welcome, contribution to public discussion about morality.

There has always been tension in the Church between those who want to hold to tradition and those who want to revise the doctrines and practices of the Church so that it remains relevant to the surrounding culture to which it wants to witness. This tension can be calm and creative, helping to restrain extremists at both ends of the spectrum and keep the Church faithful to both its roots and its mission. Sometimes, however, two different factions become polarized on a particular issue, and the tension becomes hostile and destructive. The second chapter in this section will look at the role that Virtue Ethics could play in pacifying and uniting the Church in situations like this.

> *You can appreciate both that the Bible's wisdom is a valuable asset to discussions about how to organize any society and that particular ways of behaving that are right for Christians should not be imposed by law on people who do not follow that religion.*

The present candidate for a universal ethic for the world is the ethic of human rights. Coming out of the secular democracies of the West, the idea behind this way of thinking is profoundly atheistic and, while clearly promoting the virtue of justice, is now being seen to have no way of preserving the other virtues that are needed if human society is to flourish. The last chapter of this section will consider whether Virtue Ethics could become a better candidate for a universal ethic, one that the major religions of the world, which influence the thinking of so many people, can buy into, influence, and promote.

Virtue Ethics and legislation

PEOPLE WHO ARE STRONGLY COMMITTED to either the ethics of rules or the ethics of consequences believe that these approaches are helpful in the ethical discussions that often surround the process of making laws, but how helpful can Virtue Ethics be in this process? Can an approach that focuses on ideas about good people rather than ideas about good rules or good outcomes—an approach that is so flexible and personal—be of any use here? If Christians can embrace this approach, can it make their contribution to these discussions more valuable and more welcome than the fragmented and often disregarded contributions that they presently make?

THE NEED FOR RULES

Rules are needed for the smooth running of communities, institutions, and social activities of many kinds. Driving cars on public roads, for example, must be controlled and people's property and basic freedoms must be protected. This is the role of the state.

In modern democracies, there is much discussion about how far the state does and should control the values and personal moral behavior of its citizens, and how far religious institutions should have a say in this control.

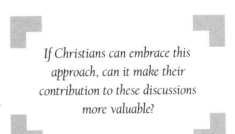

If Christians can embrace this approach, can it make their contribution to these discussions more valuable?

In many modern states, there is a fairly strong majority religion and, in some, a history of state partnership with and some measure of control by a particular religious group. Increasingly in modern times, however, secularization and immigration have led to a more mixed population, and the authority of one particular religious group to determine how people should behave is questioned. Is it right that Muslim law or Christian morality should be imposed by the state when sizable proportions of its citizens are not Muslim or Christian?

A moral revolution

In Britain, for example, with its established Christian Church, it was accepted until quite recently that the law upheld what were seen as Christian moral standards, especially in the area of sexual behavior. This assumption was, however, quickly eroded in the 1960s with a series of new laws about homosexual behavior, censorship, abortion, and divorce. While conservative Christian groups such as Mary Whitehouse's Nationwide Festival of Light opposed these moves, the Church of England supported them on the basis that while, for Christians, the standards of behavior had not changed, it was no longer appropriate for Christian standards to be imposed on the whole nation.[38]

In America the situation has always been rather different. In the context of a principle of separation of church and state, recognition of diversity, and a high view of personal freedom, there had been no sudden legal moral revolution. There is, however, still a wide range of views about how far, in a democratic state, Christian standards should be imposed on all citizens by law.

In a survey conducted in the United States in 1998, 62 percent of the Evangelical Christians questioned thought that "Christian morality should be the law of the land, even though not all Americans are Christians." A significant 45 percent of Mainline Christians agreed with them, but only 10 percent of the "nonreligious" did. When asked if they believed "religion was a private matter that should be kept out of public debate over social and political issues," 84 percent of the nonreligious category agreed, as did 48 percent of Mainline Christians, and only 25 percent of Evangelicals. Among Evangelical Christians 37 percent went further and said they agreed with the statement that "Christians need to try to change society using ways they know may cause conflict or set people against each other."[39]

Countries where there is a majority Muslim population and a democratic style of government, such as Turkey and Egypt, see the same division of views on how much religion should inform a country's laws. It is interesting that in both Egypt and Turkey the trend is toward increasing Islamization of legal and social systems.[40]

In most of the world today the trend is for societies to get increasingly diverse, with people holding, and living by, an increasing variety of worldviews. Many people conclude that, in this situation, giving people the freedom to set their own values and choose their own lifestyles is an inevitable and healthy move. But then, in the view of some commentators, things start to go wrong.

wrestling with life's tough issues

The new Virtue Ethics approaches to moral philosophy are giving people the language to explain what it is that goes awry. These approaches suggest that for a society to function well, it may not need shared moral rules, but it does need, at some level, a shared sense of values—a common view of what a good life is and what sort of people we need to be to achieve one.

When the idea that legally enforced rules should control people's moral lives was abandoned, it left a vacuum; for what will now control the moral behavior of corporations and states? Moral philosophers turned their thinking toward issues of justice and rights. People were released to live how they wanted to live, but out with the bathwater of unwelcome moral control went the baby—an appreciation, a cherishing, and a promoting of the virtues without which communities and the individuals who live in them are unlikely to flourish.

Kant thought that his theory of rationally derived moral rules could make a basis for a just and secure society, but the idea of living for duty—regulating one's life by rational, universal rules—has been rejected by the majority of people today. Mill thought that his theory of maximizing personal happiness could do the same, but pleasure has been exposed as a flimsy value on which to base a community's life. It seems that neither of these theories can provide what we need now.

> *For a society to function well, it may not need shared moral rules, but it does need, at some level, a shared sense of values—a common view of what a good life is and what sort of people we need to be to achieve one.*

Nostalgia for the virtues

If Christians could stop talking as the Pharisees did about universal moral prohibitions, or as hedonists do about love being all we need, and start focusing on virtues, they would almost certainly find people willing to listen. Amid all the ridicule of the church in the media, I perceive some nostalgia for the virtues, the character traits that make life worth living—honesty, simplicity, faithfulness, self-control, generosity. If Christians started talking about virtues again rather than about rules or consequences, their contributions could be a welcome voice against the spirit of the age. They would certainly find allies in the other religious traditions that are now well established, and I believe they might find more support than they expect from those with no religious faith.

Christians can no longer expect their moral rules to be imposed by the state, but they could, if they began to see the distinctive ethics of the New Testament in terms of the ethics of virtue, find that they have something to contribute to the process of lawmaking that is both comprehensible and welcome to their fellow citizens.

The argument that sustains the ethics of rules—that a particular category of behavior is always wrong because God tells us so in the Scriptures or because our reason leads us to see it that way—no longer carries much weight in our society at large. The argument that sustains the ethics of consequences—that all rules should be lifted and people encouraged to see that our freedom and happiness need to be balanced with the freedom and happiness of others—leaves a vacuum exactly where a society needs the most solid of foundations.

A legal system cannot be neutral on moral values; it cannot help but reflect and influence the moral values of its citizens. If these values are vague and fragmented, neither given due reflection nor articulated, the society will become like the house built on sand in Jesus' parable (Matthew 7:24–27). In a democracy, these foundations need to be agreed among its citizens, which means that in a pluralistic society there has to be discussion among people with different worldviews. The language of Virtue Ethics opens up the possibility of this sort of discussion in a new way.

The American Constitution was set up to ensure freedom for its citizens to live as they chose, so long as they did not jeopardize the freedom or safety of others. It does not, however, avoid identifying moral values or making moral judgments, because the pursuit of life, liberty, and happiness is enshrined in it. Are these the values that we, as Christians, want our society to be based on, or is there a wider debate to be engaged in among people from both religious and secular traditions?

Amid all the ridicule of the church in the media, I perceive some nostalgia for the virtues, the character traits that make life worth living—honesty, simplicity, faithfulness, self-control, generosity.

WHAT CAN CHRISTIANS CONTRIBUTE TO THIS DEBATE?

Reintroducing the language of virtues could give Christians the chance to feed into the legal process the distinctive ethics of the New Testament. We

wrestling with life's tough issues

could offer to our jaded society everything that the story of Jesus shows us about what human life can be at its best, and how communities can become places where people reach this potential.

In a pluralistic democracy, Christians and people of other religious and secular worldviews have the right and the duty to present the special insights that arise from their beliefs, but how would this work for the Christian contribution in, for example, the debate about the legalization of euthanasia?

Reintroducing the language of virtues could give Christians the chance to feed into the legal process the distinctive ethics of the New Testament.

There is clearly a lot of work to be done, but here are some preliminary thoughts. If Christians interpret their particular insights from a Virtue Ethics perspective, they will take the line that the Bible's old laws about not taking life are not absolute, universal rules: life was always more complicated than that. We can't conclude from these laws that taking one's own life, or helping someone else to take theirs, has been declared by God always to be wrong. These old laws are, however, a very useful pointer to the values and virtues that a society needs in order to function well.

On the other hand, they will not advise that Jesus' teaching about the preeminence of love means that everyone should be free to do (and get the help to do) exactly what they choose with their own lives. The Christian idea of love is richer than that. We may have the right to take our own life, but doing so may, in some circumstances, be a selfish, cruel, or cowardly action, an action that expresses and promotes vices. Helping someone else to die when they choose can, in some situations, be seen as a just and loving action, but this does not mean that making it legal would necessarily encourage the virtues that lead to flourishing communities.

Virtues from the Christian story

Christians taking a Virtue Ethics approach would rather want to think about the special values that emerge from the Christian story and see how best the law could promote these values in our society. In the euthanasia debate, surely one of the virtues that would be found significant is respect and care for the most vulnerable members of society, because the Christian story tells us that God's kindness and generosity extends to everyone at every stage of life. This is the Christian virtue that inspired the hospice movement, which has already made a remarkable difference to the end of many people's lives. A law that would make it easier for vulnerable people to lose their sense of personal worth, to be manipulated, neglected, or disposed of for the benefit of others would therefore need to be considered with great care.

Virtue Ethics approaches would then help people make the link between the virtues that inform debates about abortion and euthanasia and debates about other issues that involve the value of human life, such as the way our society treats the poor, the asylum seeker, the criminal, and its perceived enemies.

How insights like these can be built into laws is not straightforward or easy, but discussions that focus on the relevant virtues, as well as the relevant rights, seem to me to have a better chance of producing laws that lay a firm foundation for a flourishing society.

Some people may wish that lawmaking could be morally neutral, and that the rules laid down by religious institutions were not allowed to influence the law in a pluralistic secular state, but it is being increasingly realized that a society does need a shared sense of values in order to flourish. If Christians could start to see their contribution in terms of special insights about the virtues instead of special insights about rules or general happiness, they could perhaps find a more useful, just, and welcome role in the lawmaking processes of our society.

17

What can Virtue Ethics do for the Church?

WE SAW IN THE LAST chapter how coming to biblical ethics from a Virtue Ethics approach might help the Christian Church to make a useful contribution to the ethical discussions that take place in the process of lawmaking—a contribution that has a chance of being acceptable to people presently in the habit of dismissing anything that comes from the faith traditions.

It could also, I believe, help a great mass of confused Christians to reclaim the Bible as a practical, coherent, and challenging source of help to live well in today's world and, at the same time, help to resolve some of the (often hostile) divisions within the Church on ethical issues.

One of the sources of this confusion and hostility is the different ways in which Christians approach the Bible looking for ethical guidance, some looking mainly for timeless and universal rules and some looking mainly for encouragement to make love the single guiding virtue.

Those at the extreme conservative end of the Church declare that "the Bible says . . ." this or that category of actions is absolutely prohibited, and that anyone who disagrees with them is "unbiblical"—meaning that they are ignorant or in defiance of the Bible's clear teaching. These are the people who, I have suggested, are in danger of becoming like the Pharisees in the Gospel stories. They believe that "the world's agenda"—the culture in which the faith is embedded—should not be allowed to influence or divert Christians in their defense of the timeless pronouncements of God that they find in the Bible.

> *Between them, these two opposed approaches seem to me to have led to a great loss of confidence in the Bible as a guide to living well for the majority of Christians.*

Those at the extreme liberal end of the Church say that the Bible is hopelessly out of date and, in its detail, unreliable as a guide to living in today's world. They argue that Christians should take as binding only the commandment to love each other, and should then use their reason and their understanding of the world to decide how this commandment works out in particular situations. These are the people who, I have suggested, are in danger of becoming hedonists. They believe that the world's emphasis on avoiding harm and maximizing happiness should simply become the Church's agenda too.

A LOSS OF CONFIDENCE IN THE BIBLE

Between them, these two opposed approaches seem to me to have led to a great loss of confidence in the Bible as a guide to living well for the majority of Christians who stand between the two extremes and find both of them problematic and unattractive. There are many Christians who sincerely want their faith to mold their lives but do not believe that all the ethical advice we find in the Bible can be turned into timeless rules about how they should behave in every situation. Neither do they believe that love can make everything right.

So can the ideas contained in Virtue Ethics help these Christians to find a more confident and persuasive voice? I believe they can, first by demonstrating how the present polarization in the world of Christian ethics has arisen (from the fragmented moral philosophy of the modern era) and then by revealing how a return to premodern ethical thinking can lead to a challenging and flexible Christian ethic which takes seriously both the Bible's agenda and the world's agenda. Christians can then appreciate the Bible's unique ethical teaching and see that the changing values of the cultures in which they find themselves are crucially relevant to how they apply that teaching. They can respond to the call to love their neighbors and see that this involves all the Christian virtues—justice, honesty, faithfulness, and so on, as well as simply benevolence.

Can the ideas contained in Virtue Ethics help these Christians to find a more confident and persuasive voice?

An approach to the Bible that emphasizes the old idea of a virtuous life as the distinctive element in Christian ethics, rather than the modern secular ideas of universal rules or concern about consequences, allows Christians to appreciate again both the flexibility of Paul's ethics and their distinctive content. This rediscovery involves asking questions about Paul's attitude to the Jewish law and its place in Christian living.

THE ROLE OF THE LAW

The role of the Jewish law in the new Christian Church was a matter of contention in the early days. In Acts 15 we read about a church council, held probably in A.D. 49 or 50. A spokesman for the Pharisees party recommended that the Gentiles who had converted to Christianity should be circumcised and required to obey the law of Moses. After Peter, Barnabas, and Paul had spoken, reminding the council that Christians are saved by grace and telling of the wonderful things that God was doing in the Gentile church, James made a judgment. There was to be a compromise. Gentile Christians did not have to be circumcised or to keep the other laws of Moses, except for three: they were required to abstain from food polluted by idols, from sexual immorality, and from eating the meat of strangled animals and blood.

We can speculate that these requirements were added for a specific situation, in order that Jewish Christians might not be too horrified by the behavior of their fellow Christians, and within a few years Paul at least had dropped them as universal rules for Gentile Christians. We know this because, in

In the past, these laws had been seen as the means to both justification and sanctification. Now they were the means to neither. Christians are under a new covenant.

Galatians 2:11–13, Paul declares that Peter was "clearly in the wrong" when, on the arrival of James in Antioch, he drew back from his new habit of eating with Gentiles (which would have involved eating non-kosher food).

The Jewish law regulated every aspect of life from sunrise to sunset, from birth to death. According to Paul, Christian living was not to be regulated in the same way—by laws. All the ceremonial and cultic laws, all the laws about food and hygiene, festivals, use of the land, social life, and relationships were not binding on Gentile Christians.

In the past, these laws had been seen as the means to both justification and sanctification. Now they were the means to neither. Christians are under a new covenant. They are justified (counted righteous) by faith in Jesus' death for them on the cross (Romans 3:23–25), and they are sanctified (made righteous) by the work of his Spirit living in them (1 Thessalonians 2:13).

Christ as the end of the law

Paul makes the point over and over again, and in several different ways. Now that Christ has come, the law has become obsolete (Galatians 3:19); Christians are no longer "under law" (Romans 6:14; 1 Corinthians 9:20; Galatians 5:18); they are dead to the law (Romans 7:4, 6; Galatians 2:19), redeemed from the curse of the law and "no longer under the supervision of the law" (Galatians 3:13, 25); they are "released from the law" so that they no longer serve "in the old way of the written code," and "Christ is the end of the law" (Romans 7:6; 10:4).

Like Jesus, however, Paul continued to hold the Jewish law in high regard, seeing a useful role for it. It reveals God's nature and purpose to us; it shows us that God is holy and good and wants to build a community of people who enjoy him, reflect his nature, and work with him toward his purpose. The law shows us the impossibility of our becoming such a community by our own efforts (Romans 3:20; 5:13; 7:7–12). Without the law we would not know that we were in need of grace and mercy, in need of a savior (Galatians 3:24). Paul argues that the law is also good "if one uses it properly" for restraining "the ungodly and sinful, the unholy and irreligious" (1 Timothy 1:8–9).

MOVING ON TO MATURITY

Virtue Ethics recognizes the good role of rules in teaching people values and training them to be virtuous, for social control at all sorts of levels and when decisions have to be made quickly, but it also recognizes that the aim is for people to move on, for their good actions to be motivated by good character inside rather than by rules imposed from outside.

Paul also appears to believe that as Christians become mature and develop a godly wisdom, they can question rules and be flexible about applying them in specific situations or changing contexts. This is made clear when he says in 1 Corinthians 9:20–23, "To the Jews I became like a Jew, to win the Jews. To those under the law I became like one under the law (though I myself am not under the law), so as to win those under the law. To those not having the law I became like one not having the law (though I am not free from God's law but am under Christ's law), so as to win those not having the law. To the weak I became weak, to win the weak. I have become all things to all men so that by all possible means I might save some. I do all this for the sake of the gospel."

This is the only place where Paul says that he is not free from God's law— in the context of conforming to the law when it is beneficial to the gospel and not conforming to it when it is not. This is not only what Paul taught but also what he practiced: in Acts 16:1–3 we read that Paul had Timothy circumcised, whereas in Galatians 2:3–5 we see that he did not require the same of Titus in a different context.

Growing in holiness

One of the arguments used against taking the plain meaning of Paul's statements about the end of the law is that people are so blind and weak, so easily deceived and misled, that it would be far too dangerous to move from a morality based on rules to one based on developing character.

Paul is, in fact, much more concerned about the danger of slipping back to living by law. He sees and continually warns against its misuse—people thinking that they can be justified in God's sight by keeping the law (Romans 10:1–4; Galatians 2:16) or becoming satisfied with their progress toward sanctification.

Paul is not so anxious about people's ability to live well, and his confidence comes from his belief that it is the Spirit's work, not ours. This is how he sees the process by which Christians grow in holiness: God's Spirit within us gives us a new spiritual nature, and he grows his fruit in us (Galatians 5:22–23). While we remain here on earth, our new nature is in conflict with the old nature, which still remains (Romans 7:14–24). Our part in the process of becoming holy is to "live according to," "have [our] minds set on," be "led by," and "live by" the Spirit (Romans 8:5, 14; Galatians 5:16, 18, 25), and "put to death," "not gratify the desires of," the old sinful nature (Romans 8:13; Galatians 5:16).

A Virtue Ethics perspective helps Christians to see that Paul's various lists of vices (see 1 Corinthians 6:9–10; Galatians 5:19; Ephesians 5:5; 1 Timothy 1:9–11) are not a new set of universal and timeless rules: this would not be consistent with their literary or theological context. Rather, Paul uses these variable lists to describe manifestations of the old nature (vices) that have no place in the kingdom of God. Until our glorification, character traits like these will lurk in the heart of every Christian, but they are not to be tolerated or ignored.

These lists of vices emphasize the important fact that being free from the law does not mean that Christians are free to live as they like, or to be led by happy consequences alone. Paul warns people whose lives are still dominated by their "old nature" to think carefully about their membership in the kingdom and about their position before God. He teaches Christians that their behavior needs to be constrained by and measured against the virtues that mark out the new nature—virtues that reflect the holy, just, and loving character of God (see 1 Corinthians 6:6–7; Galatians 2:22–23; Ephesians 4:2–3; Colossians 3:12–15). Behavior that fails to display virtues like these, Paul judges to be unacceptable for Christians.

Identifying and applying the Christian virtues

Paul shows us, in many instances throughout his letters, how to identify and apply the virtues of the new nature in specific contexts. The Christians in Corinth wrote to him asking how they should act in a number of particular situations. He advised them on a case of incest, on use of secular law courts and of prostitutes, on marriage, on what to do about meat sacrificed to idols that then found its way into the market, on public worship, the place of women in it and appropriate dress for them when they lead it, and on gifts and relationships within the church. Seeing how he deals with these cases is invaluable as we try to apply the virtues of the new nature to our own, quite different situations and cultural contexts.

> Paul teaches Christians that their behavior needs to be constrained by and measured against the virtues that mark out the new nature—virtues that reflect the holy, just, and loving character of God.

Did Paul turn back to the Jewish law to argue for or justify his advice? If not from the law, from where else did he derive his advice? What principles did he invoke? Did he see himself laying down a new law for Christians for all times and situations?

Paul's flexible lists of the sort of behavior produced by the old and the new natures make no direct appeal to Jewish law, although they can be seen to be informed by it, as can his other advice about Christian morality. Throughout his letters there are allusions to all Ten Commandments except the instructions about the sabbath, but he does not normally quote them directly. The only place where Paul appears to make a direct appeal to the law is where he says, "Women should remain silent in the churches. They are not allowed to speak, but must be in submission, as the Law says" (1 Corinthians 14:34).

When Paul wants to back up his advice with arguments from Scripture, he turns more often to the creation story. Women must cover their heads and

wrestling with life's tough issues

learn in quietness because "man did not come from woman, but woman from man" (1 Corinthians 11:8) and "Adam was not the one deceived; it was the woman" (1 Timothy 2:14). Elsewhere, his ethical advice flows naturally from the gospel story, which provides both the motivation for and the content of godly living. There are numerous allusions to the ethical teaching of Jesus.[41] The story of how Jesus came and died for us and sent his Spirit into our hearts leads directly to virtues like love, humility, self-sacrifice, godliness, and self-control (Philippians 2:5–8; Romans 12:1–2; Titus 2:11–13). People should be faithful and controlled in their use of sex because "your body is a temple of the Holy Spirit" (1 Corinthians 6:19) and because marriage is a picture of Christ's relationship with his Church (Ephesians 5:32).

Similarly, the need to build up the church and commend the gospel to others leads Christians to virtues like consideration, flexibility, gentleness, respect, honesty, kindness, wisdom, and innocence (1 Corinthians 10:31–33; Ephesians 4:29–32; Romans 16:19; see also 1 Peter 3:15).

A principle for moral decisions

In 1 Corinthians 11:1–16, Paul discusses appropriate head covering and hairstyles for leading public worship. The alternative reading in the NIV translation, which makes this passage all about hairstyles rather than hats or veils, seems to make most sense. Whatever the advice, however, the principle seems to be the same.

Paul does not appeal to Old Testament law, although there is plenty there about hairstyles (for example, Leviticus 10:6; 19:27). He refers several times to the creation story (1 Corinthians 11: 3, 7–8), but his main argument is this: "Judge for yourselves: Is it proper for a woman to pray to God with her head uncovered? Does not the very nature of things teach you that if a man has long hair, it is a disgrace to him, but that if a woman has long hair, it is her glory? For long hair is given to her as a covering" (vv. 13–15).

The appeal here is to sensitivity to the norms and expectations of the culture in which the Corinthian Christians lived, as well as to their fellow church members. The churches were to conform to the accepted practices of the surrounding culture in this area, so as not to cause a scandal. This was surely the same principle by which the Council of Jerusalem made their decision some years earlier (Acts 15), and Paul uses it again and again in his advice to the Corinthians and the other young churches.

The same principle is also evident in his discussion about the meat in pagan markets (1 Corinthians 8). Here he makes the point clearly that there are no universal rules about this issue, even though the leaders of the Christian

Church, from the same principle of respect for the surrounding culture, had made what turned out to be a temporary rule about it at an earlier council. The Christians in Corinth were free to do as they individually or corporately decided, but, at the same time, they were to be careful that the exercise of their freedom did not "become a stumbling block to the weak" (v. 9). They were to guide their behavior not by thoughts of their own good but for the good of the whole Christian community.

In the context of their sexual relationships, Paul uses the phrase, "'Everything is permissible for me'—but not everything is beneficial" (1 Corinthians 6:12–20). Here the appeal is to the presence of the indwelling Spirit of God in the body of the believer. The behavior of Christians should not flow from the vices that Paul sees to be inconsistent with the Spirit's presence and with being part of God's kingdom (see 6:9–10) but from the virtues that the gospel story reveals and that the Spirit grows in us.

If this is correct, Paul was not laying down a new set of rules for Christian living for all times, but showing us how to apply Christian virtues in changing situations and contexts. There are two instances where Paul could be seen to be laying down a universal rule: on the subject of haircuts for men and women, he says, "If anyone wants to be contentious about this, we have no other practice—nor do the churches of God" (1 Corinthians 11:16), and on the subject of women remaining silent in the churches and being in submission, he says, "What I am writing to you is the Lord's command" (14:37).

> *Both of these "commands" are seen by almost all Christians today as examples of Paul's general advice to be sensitive and wise in the application of the Christian virtues in the interests of the gospel.*

Both of these "commands" are seen by almost all Christians today as examples of Paul's general advice to be sensitive and wise in the application of the Christian virtues in the interests of the gospel, to ask ourselves what someone with all the virtues of a Christian character would do in this situation.

It was important that the Christian church in Corinth behaved in a way that did not scandalize the local population, not because the behavior considered natural in their pagan society (the customary way for men and women to wear their hair and the accepted position of women in relation to their husbands' authority) represented God's timeless rules for the church forever, but because of their concern for the flourishing of the church and the gospel in that city at that time.

Coherence and clarity

The insights of Virtue Ethics thus help to give Paul's ethical teaching more coherence and clarity than the previous fragmented philosophical scene has done. It shows us that the law (the entire law) really is "fulfilled" or "summed up" by love, by bearing one another's burdens (Romans 13:8–10; Galatians 5:14; 6:2). Paul really does believe that "everything is permissible" for him, that against the virtues that flow from the story of Jesus "there is no law" (Galatians 5:23).

Seen from this angle, Paul's ethical teaching inspires Christians not to become self-satisfied and complacent or to concentrate their moral energy on condemning others, but to see the continual need for repentance, mercy, and grace, and for attentiveness and openness to the work of the Spirit as he grows in us the Christian virtues of sensitivity, flexibility, kindness, and wisdom.

DIFFERENT CULTURES, DIFFERENT VIEWS

Recent debates in the Church about the appropriate roles and behavior for women and for homosexuals in the Church are examples of how polarization can occur, with extremists on one side insisting that Scripture contains timeless, universal rules, and extremists on the other insisting that the Christian principle of love demands that everyone must be accepted and welcomed on equal terms in all areas of the worldwide Church.

Christians can be free positively to respect and keep fellowship with Christians who, in different cultural contexts, choose different patterns of behavior from them.

The insights of Virtue Ethics and the light they shine on Paul's ethics illuminate for us the inadequacies of both these positions and point to a way of reaching some measure of reconciliation between them. They help us to grasp the core of Paul's ethical teaching: that Christians should act in a way that expresses and promotes the Christian virtues in their own particular context, for the sake of the gospel, so that the Church and the good news of Jesus can flourish in the society in which they live. Nothing is universally banned except behavior that expresses and promotes the vices that are incompatible with the presence of God's Spirit or being part of God's kingdom—vices that, in different ways in different contexts, destroy the Church and discredit the gospel.

With this way of looking at issues, Christians can be free positively to respect and keep fellowship with Christians who, in different cultural contexts, choose different patterns of behavior from them, as long as they see in their words and actions a sensitivity to their culture and a commitment to the Christian virtues and the gospel.

A return to premodern ideas

In several areas of its life, the Christian Church is rejecting the reductionism, exclusivism, and quest for certainty that are characteristic of the modern world and is exploring the benefits of returning to premodern ways of thinking.[42] In ethics, this means rejecting attempts to reduce New Testament ethics to simple, universal rules, the assertion that this is the only way of being "biblical" and the certainty that only people who agree with us are right.

The revival of Virtue Ethics means, however, that rejecting the way of the Pharisees does not leave us with hedonism as the only alternative. The ethics of the New Testament can also be revived as a practical, challenging, flexible guide to living well, which can reflect the complexities that modern science, globalization, democracy, and pluralism bring to our lives today. It can also help Christians to see the need for respect and gentleness, generosity and mercy in their relationships with one another.

wrestling with life's tough issues

What can Virtue Ethics do for the world?

PART OF THE SHOCK OF the attack on New York's Twin Towers on September 11, 2001, was the discovery, by people in far-flung parts of the world, that there are human beings who are like them in so many ways but whose ethical thinking is incomprehensibly different. The need for some moves toward a common foundation for global ethical thinking could not have erupted more starkly into the world's consciousness.

A fact that was highlighted on September 11, and can no longer be ignored, is that the vast majority of people in the world today feel some kind of allegiance to some form of one of the world's six main religions, or are indirectly influenced by one of them through their culture. Statistics about religious affiliation are notoriously suspect, but some collected in 1998 list over three-quarters of the world's population as affiliated with one of the six main world religions.[43] How religious people do ethics is, therefore, still a matter of immense importance in the contemporary world.

The predictions of the mid-20th century, that the spread of modernism around the world would lead to religions fading away, have been proved quite wrong. Secularism is not going to be the dominant worldview of the immediate future. What the world now needs, therefore, are ideas about ethical living—how to live peaceably together so that people can discover and experience human life at its best—that bring secular and religious ideas and traditions together.

THE ETHICS OF HUMAN RIGHTS

As we have seen, the present main candidate for a common ethic for the world is the ethic of human rights, arising from modern liberal democracy and being proposed, or in some cases imposed, by the secular West.

The idea of human rights may fail at this particular hurdle because it sits very uneasily with the idea of the need for detachment from self-centeredness, which features prominently in the ethics of all the major religions, and with the idea of a holy, sovereign creator, which lies at the heart of the Semitic religions. Virtue Ethics seems a far more promising candidate for a global ethic, just because the religious thought systems of the world could buy into it and help to develop and promote it.

The notion that we could build an ethical system from the idea of human rights grew out of the work of the English philosopher John Locke (1632–1704). It could be viewed as an attempt to build a workable society without having to change people's characters.[44]

The foundational idea is that every human being has some natural rights (described in the original American Constitution as "life, liberty, and the pursuit of happiness") purely on the basis of being a member of the human race. It is proposed that these rights exist before and are independent of any state's decision to grant them to its citizens, that they are not the result of anyone's ideas, do not grow out of the values of any particular culture, and cannot be lost.

Franklin D. Roosevelt is reported to have said, in a speech to the American Congress, "Freedom from cruelty and inhuman treatment is a natural right. It is not a grace to be given or withheld at will by those temporarily in a position to assert force over a defenseless people."[45]

Secularism is not going to be the dominant worldview of the immediate future. What the world now needs, therefore, are ideas about ethical living.

The notion of human rights has been a very productive one, and it is seen to work because as people become aware of these rights, they naturally claim them—fight for them, even. Thus, the argument goes, justice is done without the need for agreement over what a good life is, or the need either to care about and contribute to the common good or to develop the character that was previously considered necessary to achieve it.

It has been hailed as the perfect ethic for modern liberal democracies, where people of different religious and secular worldviews have to live together and where one of the highest values is the freedom of individuals to live as they wish. It has achieved a great deal in liberating and empowering people all over the world.

At the same time, however, it is a profoundly atheistic system. The three Semitic religions—Judaism, Christianity, and Islam—all begin with the

wrestling with life's tough issues

same story, a story about beings who are created not with rights but with obligations to their creator and to each other. They all go on to teach that good communities are built by developing character, primarily by individuals learning (having the grace) to depose the self from the center of their feeling, thinking, and acting. Jews call it keeping God's law; Muslims call it submitting to the will of Allah; Christians call it growing in holiness.

The three great religions that began in India—Hinduism, Buddhism, and Sikhism—all come out of a system of thought that begins with Dharma, a word that has many meanings but can be described as the eternal, revealed truth about how things are, which must guide people's thoughts and actions if they and their communities are to flourish and if they are to discover the most satisfying and authentic way of being a human being. Central to most of the traditions that come from India is also the idea that this involves overcoming the domination of the ego by right thinking and right living.

Although, in modern times, people have tried to incorporate the idea of natural rights into these religions, it is so profoundly foreign to them that no one has had much success.[46]

A clash of civilizations?

Many people from the West simply assume that the ethical system founded on the idea of human rights is the only valid one there is, and that they must, for the good of humanity, impose it on every nation in the world. Many Muslims, however, perceive it as an unwarranted alien imposition, as a clash of civilizations that must be resisted at all costs. They say, if our sovereign creator has revealed his will for our lives, and if our only hope of reaching our full potential is by a humble reception of God's mercy, how can we base our ideas about living well on what we see as our "rights"?

Some Christians in the West come into conflict with the system too, when the right to free trade clashes with their understanding of what God has revealed about the observance of a holy day or his concern for the poor; when the right to equal access to employment clashes with what they see as the Bible's teaching about gender roles and sexual practices; when the right to free speech is seen to sanction blasphemy; when people claim it is everyone's right to be a bishop or work in a Christian school if they want to, to have an abortion and choose when to die, to publish anything they like, and to see what they want on public service television.

Justice may be served well, but the ancient philosophers and the followers of the world religions know that there are other virtues which are also necessary in order for societies to flourish. It may be entirely just for someone to be

what can virtue ethics do for the world?

free to have an abortion, to help someone die well, or to put their play on the stage if they want to. Having a moral right to do something, however, does not mean that in some cases it may not also be a cowardly, unkind, selfish, unwise, mean, or cruel thing to do—that it might be destructive rather than creative of a society where people can flourish.

The fact that the ethics of human rights requires no agreement on values or commitment to promoting and developing virtues may be seen as one of its main advantages in the pluralistic, democratic societies that have emerged in the modern world. As the influence of religions in the West decreases, however, this fact is now being recognized as one of its main failings also. Without efforts to promote the virtues, they wither, and as they wither, societies become less and less healthy places in which to live. The chances of people discovering life in all its fullness (John 10:10) wither with them.

> Freedom, justice, and tolerance of other people's differences can remain on the list of virtues to be promoted, but to them can be added honesty, compassion, kindness, generosity, faithfulness, responsibility, and care.

In the past, Christian values and Christian virtues have had a large influence on the culture of the West. They could do so again, but if Christians are seen neither to show nor to teach the virtues, but rather to concentrate their energies on fighting one another (mostly about whom they can exclude from what), they will become more and more marginalized and ignored.

A BETTER CANDIDATE

So, could an ethical system founded on the idea of the virtues, a system that has recently reemerged from secular moral philosophy, have a chance of becoming a better candidate for a worldwide ethic for the human race? I believe that it could. All that is good in the language of modern liberal democracy can be turned into the language of virtues. Freedom, justice, and tolerance of other people's differences can remain on the list of virtues to be promoted, but to them can be added honesty, compassion, kindness, generosity, faithfulness, responsibility, and care.

If we are to reach any sort of agreement for a worldwide system of ethics, there is, of course, a great deal of work to be done—a great deal of listening to one another across continents and cultures—and many hurdles to be overcome. One of these hurdles is that religious people will have to see that their ethical teaching can be interpreted in terms of virtues rather than absolute rules or the calculation of loving consequences. The committed Pharisees and hedonists in all the world religions will fight against this.

Another hurdle is that secularists will need to listen to the common insights of the world's religions into what ethics entails.

I suggest that these insights are firstly that the main project in human ethics is the overcoming of egoism, and secondly that, if an ethical system is to work, it needs some element of transcendence—a commitment to something bigger than and outside the self—to motivate and inspire people to live well.[47] One of the characteristics of religions is that they provide stories and rituals to make this transcendent element come alive in people's own experience.

Since secular moral philosophers tend to assume that all religious ethics are based on an ethic of duty rather than virtue, those committed to Virtue Ethics have so far not taken these two ideas very seriously. It does not seem inconceivable, however, that they can be incorporated into a Virtue Ethics approach, which may in fact both strengthen and enhance it, as well as make it a very good contender for a universal ethic for the postmodern and persistently religious world.

This book is just a start, but, as Jesus said, the tiniest of seeds can grow into a tree so big that birds can make their homes in it (Matthew 13:32). For this to happen, Christians need to take the idea back to the Bible and, as they study the Bible again from this new perspective, seek the wisdom to discern where God's Spirit is leading his Church today.

Further reading

THE FOLLOWING PHILOSOPHICAL WORKS ARE probably the best way to pursue the subject of Virtue Ethics, although they are all fairly hard work:

Gerard J. Hughes, *Aristotle on Ethics* (London: Routledge, 2001).

Alasdair MacIntyre, *A Short History of Ethics: A History of Moral Philosophy from the Homeric Age to the Twentieth Century* (London: Routledge and K. Paul, 1967; updated 1998).

Alasdair MacIntyre, *After Virtue: A Study in Moral Theory* (Notre Dame, Ind.: University of Notre Dame Press, 1981; updated 1984 and 2007).

Rosalind Hursthouse, *On Virtue Ethics* (New York: Oxford University Press, 1999).

There are two good selections of philosophical texts on Virtue Ethics:

Roger Crisp and Michael Slote, eds., *Virtue Ethics* (New York: Oxford University Press, 1997).

Daniel Statman, ed., *Virtue Ethics: A Critical Reader* (Washington, D.C.: Georgetown University Press, 1997).

For Christian responses to Virtue Ethics, you could start with:

Jean Porter, *The Recovery of Virtue: The Relevance of Aquinas for Christian Ethics* (Louisville, Ky.: Westminster John Knox Press, 1990).

Stanley Hauerwas, *A Community of Character: Toward a Constructive Christian Social Ethic* (Notre Dame, Ind.: University of Notre Dame Press, 1981).

Study guide

BELOW ARE SOME SUGGESTIONS FOR leaders wanting to study this book with a group. There is a set of tasks and questions on Section 1, "Virtue Ethics explained," and on Section 3, "Virtue Ethics evaluated," and some that can be used for each of the six stories. If you want to use the book for a short course (five or six sessions), you could pick some of the questions on Section 1 that you think most appropriate for your group, choose how many of the stories you have time for, and end with a session on Section 3. The group members could then read the other stories and themes for themselves if they wanted to.

These are subjects that can raise strongly opposed opinions. It would help if you could start by acknowledging that people will come to the study from different starting points and that you are trying to find out what the Bible says about them rather than exploring your own opinions. Start the group with prayer that God's Holy Spirit will help you to hear what the Bible is saying to you today, and encourage people to try to listen to one another with patience, humility, and self-control.

SECTION 1: VIRTUE ETHICS EXPLAINED

- What are the characteristics of "a good life"? How much do peace, prosperity, happiness, love, luck, righteousness, self-confidence, or a good character contribute to a good life?

- Look at Matthew 5:1–7. How do your ideas compare with what Jesus says here?

- How important to Jesus is character, rather than external situations, material factors, or our actions?

- Remind yourselves of the content of Matthew 5:27–48. Do you think Jesus was making a point about character here, or was he making the Jewish laws even harder to keep?

Make sure that the members of the group have read chapter 3 or are at least clear about the three ways to approach ethical questions outlined there.

- What are the advantages and disadvantages of Christians trying to answer moral dilemmas by looking in the Bible for universal, timeless moral rules? Can you find passages in the Bible that appear to encourage this approach? (Don't miss Exodus 20:1–17; Matthew 5:17–20.)

- Are some of the moral rules we find in the Old and New Testaments no longer applicable today? If so, how do we know which ones they are? Look at Leviticus 19; Acts 15:19–21; 1 Corinthians 11:11–16 for examples.

- What are the advantages and disadvantages of Christians trying to answer moral dilemmas by appealing only to the Holy Spirit's gift of love? Can you find passages in the Bible that appear to encourage this approach? (Don't miss Luke 10:25–28; Romans 13:8–10.)

- Does the Virtue Ethics approach—looking for virtues to pursue rather than rules to keep or consequences to maximize—offer a way of bringing these two approaches together without losing their advantages? Can you find passages in the Bible that appear to encourage this approach? (Don't miss Matthew 5:48; Matthew 23:23–24; Galatians 5:13–22.)

- Why do you think Christian opinion on some ethical issues (for example, women's ministry, homosexuality, war) gets so polarized? How important are the different cultures people live in? Should Christians be able to agree on a distinctive way of living that is based on the Bible? Could this incorporate flexibility for different cultures?

Section 2: Questions on the stories

You can answer the following questions for as many of the stories as your group has chosen to study. Start by recapping the story and trying to imagine yourselves either in the situation or advising someone in the situation.

- What are the most relevant facts in the story?

- Discuss your preliminary thoughts about the possible courses of action and their advantages and disadvantages.

Read the Bible passage.

- Are there different ways of interpreting the passage?

- How important is the cultural context in which the passage was written and first read?

- Are there other passages or biblical principles that need to be taken into account in making a decision in this situation?

- Can we derive any timeless, universal rules from the relevant passages? If so, to what course of action would they lead? Would this outcome be a good and loving one?

- If love is mentioned, does it imply more than wanting others to be happy? If you thought only about reaching the best consequences for everyone involved, to what course of action would you be led? Do you have any concerns about this conclusion? Are there other virtues or moral principles that need considering?

- What particular virtues does this passage encourage Christians to pursue? Which are relevant to this situation, and what course of action would be best to express and develop them? Does this seem to you a good course of action?

- If we think in terms of virtues to pursue, does this make the passage more useful in this particular situation?

- What course of action should the person in the story take if they want to mold their lives by the Bible?

- If you can't agree, can you see why and how much this matters?

SECTION 3: VIRTUE ETHICS EVALUATED

Read Matthew 7:24–27. How best can Christians contribute to laying a sound foundation for our society—prayer and mission, lobbying and campaigning, voting, working in politics or the media?

- In a democracy where people hold a range of different worldviews, how far should the state control personal moral behavior? Should Christians try to impose their standards on people who do not follow their faith, by making adultery, dishonesty, and blasphemy crimes, and denying divorces, abortions, and euthanasia to those who want them? Are there any principles that lie behind your answers to these questions?

- Does a society need a shared sense of moral values—ideas about what a good life is and what sort of person you need to be to achieve one? What happens to both individual and collective behavior if it doesn't have that shared sense?

- What special insights do Christians have to contribute to public discussion about moral values? What is it that emerges from the Christian story—a set of universal rules, inspiration to commit to general happiness, or a set of virtues to be cherished and promoted? Which of these approaches is most likely to find a response in people who do not know or follow the Christian way?

- Does the language of virtues open up the possibility of a discussion between people of different worldviews about a moral foundation for our society and give Christians the chance to feed into the legal process the distinctive ethic of the New Testament? (You could discuss how this might work in the debate about euthanasia or the treatment of immigrants, criminals, and enemies.)

Read 1 Corinthians 1:10, which is an appeal to Christians to agree with each other, to heal the divisions between them, and "be perfectly united in mind and thought."

- Do you agree that Christians today are confused and divided about how to use the Bible for making ethical decisions? Are there divisions among people equally committed to living by the Bible? What do you see as the root of this confusion and division?

- How important are "the Bible's agenda" (the gospel and its implications) and "the world's agenda" (the values of the culture in which we live)? Do we need to take them both equally seriously?

- How flexible is Paul's varied ethical advice in 1 Corinthians? What were the principles by which he encouraged Christians to decide the right thing to do? (See 6:12, 19; 8:9; 9:19–23; 10:23, 31–33.)

- Can we see Paul laying down universal rules anywhere in this letter? (See 11:14–16; 14:33–38.)

- Why do you think Paul warns us against the sort of behavior listed in 6:9–10?

- Do the insights of Virtue Ethics illuminate the inadequacies of both the ethics of rules and the ethics of consequences? Do they point to a way of reconciling the two approaches in some measure, enabling Christians to respect and keep fellowship with those who, in different cultural contexts, choose different patterns of behavior?

- What do you think the idea of natural human rights has achieved in the world, and where has it failed? Does giving everyone an equal right to happiness lead to flourishing societies and peace in the world?

- In what ways have religious people found themselves at odds with the ideas behind human rights and the legislation it has led to?

- Do the world's religions have some deeper insights about what is needed for societies to flourish?

- What virtues, in addition to justice, do you think need to be recognized and promoted for a society to flourish?

- Could Virtue Ethics have a chance of becoming a better candidate for a worldwide ethic for the human race in our postmodern and persistently religious world?

Notes

1. Richard Higginson, *Dilemmas: A Christian Approach to Moral Decision Making* (Louisville, Ky.: Westminster John Knox Press, 1988).
2. Rosalind Hursthouse explains her ideas most clearly in a paper called "Virtue Ethics and Abortion," in a book edited by Daniel Statman: *Virtue Ethics: A Critical Reader* (Washington, D.C.: Georgetown University Press, 1997).
3. See, for example, Immanuel Kant, *Critique of Pure Reason* (ed. and trans. Marcus Weigelt; London, New York: Penguin, 2007) or Immanuel Kant, *Fundamental Principles of the Metaphysics of Ethics* (8th ed., trans. Thomas Kingsmill Abbott; London: Longmans, 1920).
4. You can see this argued by Jean Porter, in *The Recovery of Virtue: The Relevance of Aquinas for Christian Ethics* (Louisville, Ky.: Westminster John Knox Press, 1990).
5. Delia Smith is a household name in England, where her cookbooks and cooking shows have been very popular since the 1970s.
6. People like Socrates (c. 469–399 B.C.), Plato (c. 428–348 B.C.), and Aristotle (384–322 B.C.).
7. You can read more about this in Alasdair MacIntyre's *A Short History of Ethics: A History of Moral Philosophy from the Homeric Age to the Twentieth Century* (2d ed.; London: Routledge, 1998).
8. J. B. Schneedwind, "The Misfortunes of Virtue," in *Virtue Ethics* (ed. Roger Crisp and Michael Slote; New York: Oxford University Press, 1997).
9. The Roman Emperor Constantine was converted to Christianity in A.D. 312.
10. The Enlightenment is the name given to new intellectual and social trends that began to develop in the late 17th century.
11. R. C. Sproul, *Ethics and the Christian* (Wheaton, Ill.: Tyndale House, 1983).
12. Ibid., 24.
13. Ibid., 48.
14. See, for example, Deuteronomy 30.
15. John Stuart Mill, *Utilitarianism* (London: Parker, Son and Bourn, 1863). I have picked out the single figure of Mill for convenience. Other philosophers were involved in the development of these forms of ethics, which are often called utilitarianism.

16. John Stuart Mill, *Utilitarianism, Liberty, and Representative Government* (London: J. M. Dent & Sons, 1948), 9.

17. Joseph F. Fletcher, *Situation Ethics: The New Morality* (Philadelphia: Westminster Press, 1966).

18. John A. T. Robinson, *Honest to God* (London: SCM Press, 1963), 116. See also Robinson's later book, *Christian Freedom in a Permissive Society* (London: SCM Press, 1970).

19. *The Alternative Service Book 1980* (London: SPCK; Cambridge: Cambridge University Press, 1980), 130. Thomas Cranmer served as Archbishop of Canterbury during the reigns of King Henry VIII and King Edward VI. He is thought to have compiled and revised the *Book of Common Prayer*, used widely in the Church of England.

20. Elizabeth Anscombe, "Modern Moral Philosophy," *Philosophy* 33 (1958), 1–19.

21. See Daniel Statman, ed., *Virtue Ethics: A Critical Reader* (Washington, D.C.: Georgetown University Press, 1997).

22. See, for example, John Bowker's introduction to *Making Moral Decisions* (ed. Jean Holm with John Bowker; London: Pinter, 1994).

23. I will not refer to individual philosophers or their various writings. If you would like to follow these up, you could refer to two collections of papers on the subject: Daniel Statman, ed., *Virtue Ethics: A Critical Reader* (Washington, D.C.: Georgetown University Press, 1997), and Roger Crisp and Michael Slote, eds., *Virtue Ethics* (New York: Oxford University Press, 1997).

24. You can see Virtue Ethics being applied to these subjects in the two collections of papers mentioned earlier in this chapter and in William F. May, "The Virtues and Vices of the Elderly," in *The Patient's Ordeal* (Bloomington, Ind.: Indiana University Press, 1991).

25. One of Alasdair MacIntyre's most influential books is *After Virtue: A Study in Moral Theory* (Notre Dame, Ind.: University of Notre Dame Press, 1981; updated 1984 and 2007).

26. Alasdair MacIntyre, *A Short History of Ethics: A History of Moral Philosophy from the Homeric Age to the Twentieth Century* (London: Routledge and K. Paul, 1967; updated 1998).

27. Stanley Hauerwas, *A Community of Character: Toward a Constructive Christian Social Ethic* (Notre Dame, Ind.: University of Notre Dame Press, 1981).

28. John Barton, "Virtue in the Bible," *Studies in Christian Ethics* 12 (1999): 13.

29. Ibid., 18.

30. Ibid., 22. Readers interested in following up Christian responses to Virtue Ethics could start with the introduction to Jean Porter's *The Recovery of Virtue: The Relevance of Aquinas for Christian Ethics* (Louisville, Ky.: Westminster John Knox Press, 1990).

31. Stories would include Cornelius Ryn, *The Longest Day: June 6, 1944* (New York: Simon and Schuster, 1959), which was made into a film by Darryl F. Zanuck in 1962, and the film *The Battle of Britain*, produced by S. Benjamin Fisz et al. in 1969. Secular rituals include Remembrance Day in Britain and Veterans' Day in the United States.

32. If you would like to read a commentary on this subject, you could get hold of David Instone-Brewer, *Divorce and Remarriage in the Bible: The Social and Literary Context* (Grand Rapids, Mich.: Eerdmans, 2002).

33. In 1959 the Archbishop of Canterbury instituted a study and as a consequence, recommended that suicide no longer be considered a crime and proposed that a new, alternative burial service be written for people who had killed themselves (Church of England General Assembly Board for Social Responsibility [1959], "Ought Suicide to be a Crime?" Church of England Information Office).

34. Usually taken to include Proverbs, Ecclesiastes, Job, some Psalms, some of Jesus' teaching, and the letter of James.

35. See chapter 2.

36. See, for example, Michael Slote, "From Morality to Virtue," in *Virtue Ethics: A Critical Reader* (ed. Daniel Statman; Washington, D.C.: Georgetown University Press, 1997), 128–44.

37. You can also see this view expressed by John R. W. Stott in *The Message of Romans: God's Good News for the World* (Downers Grove, Ill.: InterVarsity Press, 1994), 350.

38. You can read more about this in Gerald Parsons, ed., "Between Law and Licence," in *The Growth of Religious Diversity: Britain from 1945* (New York: Routledge, in association with the Open University, 1994).

39. Christian Smith, "American Evangelicalism Embattled," in *Global Religious Movements in Regional Context* (ed. John Wolff; Burlington, Vt.: Ashgate, 2002).

40. David Herbert, "Representing Islam: The 'Islamization' of Egyptian society," in *From Sacred Text to Internet* (ed. Gwilym Beckerlegge; Burlington, Vt.: Ashgate; Milton Keynes: Open University, 2001).

41. John Stott points out fourteen of these in Romans 12–15. See *The Message of Romans: God's Good News for the World* (Downers Grove, Ill.: InterVarsity Press, 1994).

42. See, for example, Brian McLaren, *A Generous Orthodoxy: Why I Am a Missional, Evangelical, Post/Protestant, Liberal/Conservative, Mystical/Poetic, Biblical, Charismatic/Contemplative, Fundamentalist/Calvinist, Anabaptist/Anglican, Methodist, Catholic, Green, Incarnational, Depressed-yet-Hopeful, Emergent, Unfinished Christian* (El Cajon, Calif.: Youth Specialties, 2004).

43. These are the three Semitic religions—Judaism, Christianity, and Islam—and the three "Indian" religions—Hinduism, Buddhism, and Sikhism. The statistics are from *Atlas of the World's Religions* (ed. Ninian Smart; New York: Oxford University Press, 1999).

44. This is argued by Ernest L. Fortin, and you can read about it in a collection of his essays: *Human Rights, Virtue and the Common Good: Untimely Meditations on Religion and Politics* (ed. J. Brian Benestad; Lanham, Md.: Rowman & Littlefield, 1996).

45. Franklin D. Roosevelt to Congress, June 20, 1941.

46. The Roman Catholic Church tried in a document called *Rerum novarum* in 1891, and you can read about attempts in the Muslim world in David Herbert,

"Islam and Human Rights," *Religion and Social Transformations* (Burlington, Vt.: Ashgate, in association with the Open University, 2001).

47. This is argued well by Iris Murdoch in *The Sovereignty of Good* (London: Routledge and K. Paul, 1970), 74–76. The organization Alcoholics Anonymous has some interesting insights here too. See www.aa.org.

wrestling with life's tough issues